HARLEM Duet

HARLEM Duet

Djanet Sears

Harlem Duet
first published 1997 by
Scirocco Drama
An imprint of J. Gordon Shillingford Publishing Inc.
© 1996 Djanet Sears
5th printing November, 2008

Scirocco Drama Editor: Dave Carley
Cover design by Terry Gallagher/Doowah Design Inc.
Cover illustration by W. Edwards
Author photo by Tim Leyes
Production photos by Cylla Von Tiedemann
Printed and bound in Canada

We acknowledge the financial support of the Manitoba Arts Council, The Canada Council for the Arts and the Government of Canada through the Book Publishing Industry Development Program (BPIDP) for our publishing program.

Production inquiries should be addressed to:
John Rait, A.C.I., 205 Ontario Street, Toronto, ON M5A 2V6
All other enquiries should be addressed to:
Playwrights Union of Canada
54 Wolseley St., 2nd Floor, Toronto, ON M5T 1A5

Library and Archives Canada Cataloguing in Publication

Sears, Djanet
    Harlem duet
  A play.
  ISBN 1-896239-27-7
    I. Title.
PS8587.E23H37 1997   C812'.54   C97-901003-9
PR9199.3.S383H37 1997

J. Gordon Shillingford Publishing
P.O. Box 86, RPO Corydon Avenue, Winnipeg, MB Canada R3M 3S3

To Winnifred, Quisbert, Rosemarie, Terese, Celia,
Mark, Milton, Sharon, Donald, Qwyn, Kyla, Vanessa,
Djustice, Donny, Sherie and Danielle.

Acknowledgements

The Ancestors, Babara Ackerman, Lillian Allen, Anji, Arcadia
Housing Co-op, b current, Maxine Bailey, Bob Baker, Barbara
Barnes Hopkins, Bonnie Beacher, Tyrone Benskin, Ellen Bethea,
Laura Bennett, Paul Bettis, Allen Booth, Marty Bragg, Yvonne
Brewster, Talawa Theatre, Candace Burley, Steven Bush, Niomi
Campbell, The Canada Council for the Arts/U.S./Mexico
Artists Residency Program, The Canadian Stage Company,
The Chalmers Family, Clarissa Chandler, David Collins, Maria
Costa, Julie Crooks, Carolin Crumpackr, Charlotte Dean,
Michelyn Emmelle, Oni Faida Lamply, Shirley Fishman, Cheryl
Francis, Peter Freund, Michael Holness, Nalo Hopkinson, Doug
Innes, Starr Jacobs, Astrid Janson, Herbert Johnson, Monica Lee
Johnson, Jeff Jones, The Joseph Papp Public Theatre, Shelby
Jiggets, Shelby Jiggets, Ricardo Khan, Crossroads Theatre,
James King, Martin Luther King, Pia Kleber, Pat Kogan, Leslie
Lester, Roy Lewis, Kate Lushington, Alisa Palmer, Alicia Payne,
Soraya Peerbaye, ahdri zhina mandiela, Clem Marshall, Marva,
Sharon Massey, Judy McKinley, Monique Mojica, National
Endowment for the Arts, New York University: Bobst Library,
Mark Nicholson, Nightwood Theatre, Ontario Arts Council,
O.F.D.C., Andrea Ottey, Mark Owen, Jonathan Peck, Janis Pono,
Teresa Przybylski, John Rait, Otis Richmond, Dawn Roach,
Diane Roberts, Richard Rose, Viveen Scarlett, The Schomberg
Center for Research in Black Culture, Lorraine Scott, Alison
Sealy-Smith, Quisbert, Winnie, Rosie, Therese, Celia & Milton
Sears, Satori Shakor, Barb Singer, Tarragon Theatre, Kunle
Vristosw, Leslie Wilkinson, Lionel Williams, Nigel Shawn
Williams, Myra L. Taylor, Neil Thelse, Lisa Tobias, Toronto
Arts Council, Iris Turcott, Karen Tyrell, Gloria Wade Gayles,
"Inquisition", Donna Walker-Collins, Winsom, George C.
Wolfe, Ollie Woods, and Malcolm X.

Production Credits

Harlem Duet premiered on April 24, 1997, as a Nightwood Theatre production, at the Tarragon Extra Space, Toronto, Canada, with the following cast:

BILLIE .... Alison Sealy-Smith
OTHELLO ....Nigel Shawn Williams
MAGI .... Barbara Barnes Hopkins
AMAH/MONA.. Dawn Roach
CANADA .... Jeff Jones

Double Bass.. Lionel Williams
Cello ....Doug Innes

Directed by Djanet Sears
Set and costume design by Teresa Przybylski
Lighting design by Lesley Wilkinson
Music composition and arrangement by Lionel Williams
Music and sound design by Allen Booth
Assistant Director: Maxine Bailey
Stage Manager: Cheryl Francis
Assistant Stage Manager: Andrea Ottley
Dramaturgy by Diane Roberts and Kate Lushington

This production of *Harlem Duet* won four 1997 Dora Mavor Moore awards, including Best New Play (Djanet Sears); Best Direction (Djanet Sears); Best Female Performance (Alison Sealy-Smith); and Best Production (Nightwood Theatre).

Nightwood Theatre is Canada's oldest professional feminist theatre company. Founded in 1979, Nightwood Theatre has produced and developed many critically acclaimed plays, including Ann-Marie MacDonald's *Good-night Desdemona (Good-morning Juliet)*, Monique Mojica's *Princess Pocahontas and the Blue Spots*, and Susan G. Cole's *A Fertile Imagination*.

Djanet Sears

Djanet Sears is a Toronto playwright, director and actor. She is the author of the highly acclaimed *Afrika Solo*, which has toured extensively and was broadcast on CBC Radio's *Morningside*. *Afrika Solo* was published in 1990 by Sister Vision Press. *Harlem Duet*, originally workshopped at New York City's Joseph Papp Public Theatre, was produced by Toronto's Nightwood Theatre and premiered at the Tarragon Theatre in April, 1997.

nOTES oF a cOLOURED gIRL

32 sHORT rEASONS wHY i wRITE fOR tHE tHEATRE

by Djanet Sears

1   Carved from that same tree
in another age
counsel/warriors who
in the mother tongue
made drums talk
now in another tongue
make words to walk in rhythm
'cross the printed page
carved from that same tree
in another age

Khephra
Talking Drums #1 ^(Khephra 125)

2 Two years ago I found myself speaking with esteemed writer and Nobel laureate, Derek Walcott, about an upcoming staged reading I was directing of his play, *A Branch of the Blue Nile*. Toward the end of our conversation I politely requested an opportunity to ask him, what I termed, a stupid question. His eyebrows seemed to crawl up to his hairline, but he didn't say no. Not that I gave him a chance. Swiftly managing to kick all second thoughts out of my mind, I boldly asked him to tell me why he wrote. He retreated to the back of his seat, and after several long moments of pondering, he replied, "I don't know." He said that writing really wasn't a choice for him. From as far back as he could recall, he had written.

He described it as a type of organic urge. He didn't know why he wrote, but when he experienced this urge, he felt compelled to act on it. Be it on a plane, first thing in the morning, or last thing at night.

3 From as far back as I can recall, I never believed in miracles. My life had taught me not to. Then I witnessed the birth of my sister's daughter. I'd seen birth films. I'd even studied human reproduction at the undergraduate level. But this child came out of my sister—already alive. I mean, not yet fully born, her head alone protruding from between her mother's legs, she wailed. Full of voice, she slipped out of the velvety darkness that was her mother's womb, into the light. I was overcome. I watched as this tiny, golden-umber coloured soul, caught by an opaque rubber gloved doctor, in a white coat, was separated from the placenta and bundled into blanched cloth. I stood there for a moment and wondered how she would come to know of herself, blinded by the glare of snow? What would this fair world tell her? I experienced such a sadness for her—or maybe it was for myself. I wanted something different for her.

4 I wanted there to be no question of her right to take up space on this planet.

5 I was already eighteen when I saw Ntozake Shange's *For Coloured Girls Who Have Considered Suicide When The Rainbow Is Enuf* in New York City. This was the first live stage production by a writer of African descent I had ever seen. **6** This will not be Qwyn's fate. **7** She must have access to a choir of African voices, chanting a multiplicity of African experiences. One voice does not a chorus make. And I will not wait. **8** I harbour deep within me tales that I've never seen told. **9** I too must become an organ and add my perspective, my lens, my stories, to the ever growing body of work by and about people of African descent.

10 Thirty-seven years ago, and nine months before I was born, in a country over three thousand miles away, Lorraine Hansberry began rehearsals for her first play. In the season of my birth, *Raisin in the Sun* opened to extraordinary critical and popular acclaim.

11 ...*Raisin in the Sun* marked a turning point, for until this time no black writer, black actor, black director, or technician had benefited financially from any of the plays about black people that had been presented (in the commercial theatre).(King vii)

12 An old West African proverb states that, as a people, we stand on the shoulders of our ancestors. **13** Lorraine Hansberry is my mother—in the theatre—and she accompanies me wherever I go. **14** I have been known to drop her a few lines, now and then. **15** Yes, she responds. **16** As a woman of African descent, and a writer for the stage, I stand on her shoulders. They are a firm and formidable foundation on which to rest my large and awkward feet.

17 Acting is a craft that I have been called to by my nature. Writing is a craft that I have chosen to nurture. **18** As a young actor, I soon realized that a majority of the roles that I would be offered did not portray me in the way I saw myself, my family, or my friends, in life. I became consumed by my own complaining. **19** Complaining, imploring, and protesting only served to disperse my energy.

20 Protest takes an enormous toll. We can and should make noise; however, in most cases our screams fall upon deaf ears.

21 Don't get me wrong here, without protest we'd never have had the likes of Martin, Malcolm, or Angela. Activism is a craft in and of itself. My skills are as a theatre practitioner, and this is the medium I must use.

That's why I am so impressed by artists like Baraka, Sanchez, Bullins, Caldwell, Hansberry, Baldwin, Giovanni, Milner, and Ahmad, many of whom were involved in the Black Arts Movement of the 1960's. The fact is they used their work as a vehicle with which to express personal and political passions.

22 In early 1993, Christine Moynihan approached me, on behalf of the Toronto Theatre Alliance and Equity Showcase Productions, about coordinating the spring 'Loon Cafe' (a one-off evening of presentations involving a host of performers, directors, writers, production workers, designers and supporters). I agreed, on the condition that I could do anything. In the ensuing weeks I developed the blueprint for the evening which I titled: *Negrophilia: An African American Retrospective: 1959-1971.* The three studio spaces of Equity Showcase were renamed Obsidian, Onyx and Jet. And the events taking place, three in each room over the course of the evening, involved readings, performances and discussions around Black theatre in America. There were plays that I had loved and had only read. One new piece, *Jimmy and Lolo*, was a collaboration, based on an idea that had been brewing inside of me for ages. Performed on the rooftop of an adjacent building, the play tells the story of the relationship between James Baldwin and Lorraine Hansberry.

The entire event was inspirational; a rousing celebration of Blackness.

23 I have a dream. A dream that one day in the city where I live, at any given time of the year, I will be able to find at least one play that is filled with people who look like me, telling stories about me, my family, my friends, my community. For most people of European descent, this is a privilege they take for granted.

24 Like Derek Walcott, I too have no choice. I must write my own work for the theatre. I must produce my own work, and the work of other writers of African descent. Then my nieces' experience of this world will almost certainly be different from my own.
25 But where do I start? How do I find the words?

26 My good friend Clarissa Chandler, a business consultant, educator, and motivational speaker, shared with me a process for using my nagging mind and raging heart, as a way to get back in touch with my innermost knowing and creative desires. She identified three steps of transformation that I could use like footprints leading me back home.

27 First: identify the place of complaint. (This can sometimes be evident in the complaining we do in hiding, in conversation with friends, and/or in the privacy of our own minds.) Second: Say it out loud. Create a mantra out of it. (Give it room in the world). Third: locate a creative point of expression for this mantra. **28** Paint it, dance it, sculpt it, or write about it. Why limit yourself?

29 As a veteran theatre practitioner of African Descent, Shakespeare's *Othello* had haunted me since I first was introduced to him. Sir Laurence Olivier in black-face. Othello is the the first African portrayed in the annals of western dramatic literature. In an effort to exorcise this ghost, I have written *Harlem Duet*. *Harlem Duet*, a rhapsodic blues tragedy, explores the effects of race and sex on the lives of people of African descent. It is a tale of love.

A tale of Othello and his first wife, Billie. Set in 1860, 1928 and contemporary Harlem at the corner of Malcolm X and Martin Luther King Boulevards, this is Billie's story. The exorcism begins.

30 For the many like me, black and female, it is imperative that our writing begin to recreate our histories and our myths, as well as integrate the most painful of experiences...[Philip 25] Writing for me is a labour of love, probably not unlike the experience of giving birth. In a very deep way, I feel that I am in the process of giving birth to myself. Writing for the stage allows me a process to dream myself into existence.

31 In a recent clinical study at Duke University researchers found that racist comments can not only lead directly to an overworked heart, but the internal stress caused by racism was found to tear the lining of blood vessels. I must write to save my own life.

32 There are a great many times when I forget. I forget why I'm doing this. Days when the blues move from a deep cerulean to icy cold pale. So I have the following words by Langston Hughes from "Note on Commercial Theatre", on my wall, just above my desk, for those times when I most need reminding.

SOMEDAY SOMEBODY'LL
STAND UP AND TALK ABOUT ME,
AND WRITE ABOUT ME—
BLACK AND BEAUTIFUL
AND SING ABOUT ME,
AND PUT ON PLAYS ABOUT ME!
I RECKON IT'LL BE
ME MYSELF!

YES, IT'LL BE ME.

Works Cited

Franklin, Deborah, Lehrman, Sally & Mason, Michael. "Vital Signs: Racism Hurts the Heart Twice." *Health*. Vol. 10, No. 4. (October, 1996)

Hughes, Langston. Excerpt from "Note on Commercial Theatre." *Selected Poems Langston Hughes*. (New York: Random House, Inc., 1974), p. 190

Khephra. "Talking Drums #1. *Essence Magazine*. Vol. 20, No. 11. (March 1990)

King, Woodie & Ron Milner. "Evolution of a People's Theatre." *Black Drama Anthology*. (New York: Signet, 1971)

Philip, Marlene. *She Tries Her Tongue*. (Charlottetown: Ragweed Press, 1989)

Characters

OTHELLO: a man of 40, present day
HE: Othello, 1928
HIM: Othello, 1860

BILLIE: a woman of 37, present day
SHE: Billie, 1928
HER: Billie, 1860

CANADA: Billie's father, 67

AMAH: Billie's sister-in-law, 33

MAGI: the landlady, 41

MONA: White, 30s (an off-stage voice)

Setting

Late summer.

Harlem: 1928, a tiny dressing room.

Harlem: the present, an apartment in a renovated brownstone, at the corner of Martin Luther King and Malcolm X boulevards (125th & Lennox)

Harlem: 1860, on the steps to a blacksmith's forge

Style note: Ellipsis marks vary; this is intentional.

...That handkerchief

Did an Egyptian to my mother give.

She was a charmer...

There's magic in the web of it.

A sibyl...in her prophetic fury sewed the work.

William Shakespeare, *Othello* (3.4.57-74)

ACT I

Prologue

(Harlem, 1928: late summer — night. As the lights fade to black, the cello and the bass call and respond to a heaving melancholic blues. Martin Luther King's voice accompanies them. He seems to sing his dream in a slow polyrhythmic improvisation, as he reaches the climax of that now famous speech given at the March on Washington. Lights up on a couple in a tiny dressing room. SHE is holding a large white silk handkerchief, spotted with ripe strawberries. She looks at HE as if searching for something. He has lathered his face and is slowly erasing the day's stubble with a straight razor. She looks down at the handkerchief.)

SHE: We keep doing this don't we?

HE: I love you… But—

SHE: Remember… Remember when you gave this to me? Your mother's handkerchief. There's magic in the web of it. Little strawberries. It's so beautiful—delicate. You kissed my fingers…and with each kiss a new promise you made…swore yourself to me… for all eternity…remember?

HE: Yes. Yes…I remember.

(Pause.)

SHE: Harlem's the place to be now. Everyone who's anyone is coming here now. It's our time. In our place. It's what we've always dreamed of…isn't it?

HE: Yes.

SHE: You love her?

HE: I...I wish—

SHE: Have you sung to her at twilight?

HE: Yes.

SHE: Does your blood call out her name?

HE: Yes.

SHE: Do you finger feed her berries dipped in dark and luscious sweets?

HE: Yes.

SHE: Have you built her a crystal palace to refract her image like a thousand mirrors in your veins?

HE: Yes.

SHE: Do you let her sip nectar kisses from a cup of jade studded bronze from your immortal parts?

HE: Yes.

SHE: Does she make your thoughts and dreams and sighs, wishes and tears, ache sweet as you can bear?

HE: Yes.

SHE: Do you prepare her bed, deep in fragrant posies, rosemary, forget-me-nots and roses, anoint her feet with civet oil, lotus musk and perfumes, place them in gossamer slippers with coral clasps, amber beads and buckles of the purest gold, kiss her ankles and knees, caress her fragrant flower, gently unfolding each petal in search of the pearl in her velvet crown?

HE: Yes.

SHE: You love her.

HE: Yes. Yes. Yes.

(He wipes his face with a towel. She stares at the handkerchief laying in her bare hand.)

SHE: Is she White?

(Silence.)

Othello?

(Silence.)

She's White.

(Silence.)

Othello...

(She holds the handkerchief out to him. He does not take it. She lets it fall at his feet. After a few moments, he picks it up.)

Scene 1

(Harlem, present: late summer — morning. The strings thump out an urban melody blues/jazz riff, accompanied by the voice of Malcolm X, speaking about the nightmare of race in America and the need to build strong Black communities.

MAGI is on the fire escape, leaning on the railing, reading a magazine with a large picture of a blonde woman on the cover. As the sound fades, she closes the magazine, surveying the action on the street below.)

MAGI: Sun up in Harlem. *(She spots the postman.)* Morning Mr. P.! Don't bring me no bill now—I warned ya before, I'm having a baby. Don't need to get myself all worked up, given my condition… I'm gonna have me a Virgo baby, makes me due 'bout this time next year… I can count. I just haven't chosen the actual father/husband candidate as yet. Gotta find me a man to play his part. I wanna conceive in the middle of December, so I've booked the Convent Avenue Baptist church for this Saturday. The wedding's at three. You sure look to be the marrying kind. What you up to this weekend, yourself sweetness? Oh well then, wish your wife well for me. Package from where? California? Oohh. Yeh, yeh, yeh. I'll be right— Hey, hey, Amah girl… Up here… Let yourself in… *(She throws a set of keys down to AMAH.)* Mr. P., give that young lady the package… Yeh, she'll bring it up for me. *(Beat.)* Thank you, sugar. *(Beat.)* You have yourself a nice day now. Alright, sweetness. Mmn, mmn, mmn!

(AMAH unlocks the door, enters and makes her way to the fire escape.)

AMAH: Magi, look at you, out on the terrace, watching the

summer blossoms on the corner of Malcolm X and Martin Luther King Boulevards.

MAGI: Nothing but weeds growing in the Soweto of America, honey. *(Shouting out.)* Billie!

AMAH: Where is she?

MAGI: I didn't want to wake her up 'till you got here. She didn't get to sleep 'till early morning. I could hear her wailing all the way downstairs.

AMAH: I can see a week. A couple of weeks at the most. But what is this?

MAGI: Two months—it's not like she's certifiable though.

(Shouting gently to BILLIE in the bedroom.)

Billie! Billie, Amah's here!

AMAH: Well, least she sleeps now.

MAGI: She's stillness itself. Buried under that ocean of self help books, like it's a tomb. Like a pyramid over her. Over the bed. *(Calling out once more.)*

Billie!

(BILLIE's body moves slightly and an arm listlessly carves its way to the surface, shifting the tomb of books, several dropping to the floor.

MAGI and AMAH make their way inside. On a large table is a vase filled with blossoming cotton branches. There is also a myriad of bottles and bags, and a Soxhlet extraction apparatus: flask, extractor and thimble, condenser, siphoning hoses, all held up by two metal stands. A Bunsen burner is placed under the flask.)

I'm just making her some coffee, can I get you a cup?

(AMAH inspects the table and searches for a space to put the small package.)

AMAH: Thanks Magi. Where d'you want this? It looks like a science lab in here.

MAGI:	Some healing concoction I've been helping her make—but she's way ahead of me these days. She's got a real talent for herbs, you know. She's been sending away for ingredients—I can't even figure out what most of them are—put the package down anywhere.
AMAH:	If I can find a space.
MAGI:	Right there. On top of that alchemy book—right in the middle. Yeh. Thanks for doing this Amah. For coming. It'll make her feel like a million dollars again.
AMAH:	Please. Billie and me go so far back, way before Andrew. Besides, sister-in-laws are family too, you know. Jenny's been simply begging to come and see her, you know, for their once a week thing. They eat sausages, mashed potatoes, and corn. Some Canadian delicacy I guess—
MAGI:	Aren't you guys vegetarians?
AMAH:	Vegan.
MAGI:	Vegan?
AMAH:	We don't eat anything that has eyes. The sausages are tofu. You know they eat exactly the same thing every time. I was glad for the break. I guess I was kinda…well…it bugged me. Jenny's always full of Auntie Billie this, Auntie Billie that. Now I miss our one night a week without her. I mean—our time alone. And I see how it's a kind of security for her.
MAGI:	Security for who?
AMAH:	Oh, I can't rent your ground floor. They won't give me any insurance 'cause I don't have a licence. And I can't get a licence until I get a cosmetician's certificate. And I can't get a cosmetician's certificate until I finish this two year course on how to do White people's hair and make-up. I told them ain't no White people in Harlem. I'd learn how to do work with chemical relaxers and Jheri curls. Now, I do dreadlocks. And do they teach that? Oh

no. They're just cracking down on people who do hair in private homes—something about lost tax revenues. I don't know... I want my own salon so bad I can taste it. 'The Lock Smiths'.

MAGI: 'The Lock Smiths'.

AMAH: Billie's supposed to be helping me with the business plan. Besides we've started trying for kid number 2. I need the space.

MAGI: You're trying?

AMAH: I'm 10 days late.

MAGI: No!

AMAH: It's still early. Don't tell Billie...you know. I'll tell her.

MAGI: Good for you, girl! Did I tell you I was having a baby?

AMAH: Oh yeh. How was he, that new candidate you were telling me about... Warren, no Waldo—

MAGI: Wendel? Wedded Wendel as I've discovered

AMAH: He didn't tell—

MAGI: Oh no. He believes that the nuclear family is the basis for a healthy society. That's why he's married. He keeps his own personal nuclear family at home in the event that he might someday want to spend time with it.

AMAH: Why'd you stop seeing George. I liked George.

MAGI: Well I liked him too.

AMAH: You two looked pretty serious there for a while.

MAGI: We'd been seeing each other the better part of... ... what...two years. I'm just not getting any younger. I mean, I kept dropping hints I was ready for him to pop the question. Seems like he don't know what question I'm referring to. So I decided to give him some encouragement. See, I've been

collecting things for my trousseau, and I have this
negligee...all white, long, beautiful lacy thing.
Looks like a see-through wedding gown. So, I'm
out on my balcony—you know, 'cause it's too hot
inside, and I still ain't got around to putting in air
conditioning. Anyway, I see him coming up the
street. So I rush in and put on the wedding dress
negligée, thinking, he'll see me in it, all beautiful
like—want to pop the question, you know. So I
open the door, me in the negligée, and he... He
stands there. Mouth wide open. And he says, he
guess he should go get a bottle of wine, seeing how
this was gonna be some kind of special occasion
an' all. Now I don't know whether he got lost...or
drunk... But I ain't seen or heard from him since.

AMAH:　　　Aahh nooo.

MAGI:　　　I should have margarined his butt when I had the
chance.

AMAH:　　　Margarined his backside?

MAGI:　　　If you want to bind a man—

AMAH:　　　You don't mean, what I think you mean?

MAGI:　　　If you want to keep a man then, you rub his
backside with margarine.

AMAH:　　　And it works?

MAGI:　　　I don't know. When I'd remember, I could never
figure out how to get from the bed to the refrigerator.

AMAH:　　　Margarine, huh?

MAGI:　　　But you've got to be careful. He might be a fool. You
don't want to be dragging no damn fool behind you
the rest of your days.

AMAH:　　　You're a regular charmer, girl.

MAGI:　　　Don't get me wrong. I don't cut the heads off
chickens, or anything now.

AMAH:　　　You know, a Jamaican lady told me about one

where you rinse your underwear and use the dirty water to cook the meal.

MAGI: Nooo! Really?

AMAH: Really.

MAGI: Ooh, I like that. Boil down some greens in panty stock. Hmm!

AMAH: Once I buried his socks under the blackberry bush by the front door. Sure enough, he always finds his way back home.

MAGI: How is True Drew?

AMAH: Oh, Andrew's real good. You know him. He was up here 'till late, night before last, even, playing broad shouldered brother.

MAGI: Yep, he's a good man. They're rare. And he went all the way down to D.C. for the Million Man March. Yeh, he's one in a million. If you ever think of trading him in…

AMAH: Don't even think about it!

MAGI: Can't blame a girl for trying. *(Calling out again.)* Billie! Billie you up yet?

(MAGI gets no response. She goes into the bedroom.)

Billie? Billie, sorry to wake you, but Amah's here. She waiting.

(BILLIE emerges . We recognize her as the woman in the prologue. She slowly makes her way to the edge of the bed.)

BILLIE: If I could only stop dreaming, I might be able to get some rest.

MAGI: You should jot them down. They're messages from other realms, you know.

BILLIE: Jenny's in a large white room—the walls start pressing in all around her…

MAGI: You OK?

BILLIE: Mm mm. Yeh. I'm fine. I'm good.

MAGI: *(Gently.)* Come on sweetheart, Amah's waiting.

BILLIE: Let me just wash my face, and my mouth.

               (MAGI leaves BILLIE to join AMAH, who is now on the fire escape.)

MAGI: She's coming…

               (AMAH hands MAGI a cup of coffee.)

               Ooh… Thanks.

AMAH: How is she?

MAGI: Better. Dreaming hard, though. Like she's on some archeological dig of the unconscious mind.

AMAH: His words hit her hard, huh.

MAGI: Like a baseball bat hits a mango. Like he was trying for a home run or something. The bat breaks through the skin, smashing the amber flesh, propelling her core out of the park, into the clouds. And she lays there, floating.

AMAH: Feeling sorry for herself.

MAGI: A discarded fruit sitting in a dish, surrounded by its own ripening mould.

AMAH: She feels so much.

MAGI: Yeh. Each of her emotions sprout new roots, long, tangled things, intersecting each other like strangle weed.

AMAH: She should go out though, get some fresh air once in a while.

MAGI: She does. Her trips out into the real world are brief, though. The grocer's for tubs of things you add water to, she calls food; the pharmacy for the pills, and the bookstore. All her money goes up in smokes and writings that tell her she really ain't out of her mind. They'd make her feel better, more beautiful, more well, until she'd see some nice chocolate brown-skinned man, dangling his prize in front of her. 'Cause all the rot inside her would begin to boil, threaten to shoot out. So she comes home, takes some pills and sleeps again that fitful sleep 'till she wakes.

AMAH: So she knows?

MAGI: Ooh she knows. She knows she's still up there in the clouds.

AMAH: She never used to be like that, you know, about colour.

MAGI: Guess it ain't never been personal before.

AMAH: But it seems bigger than that...

MAGI: Girl, you've been married what...six years?

AMAH: Seven this February coming...

MAGI: How'd you feel if Drew just upped and left you?

AMAH: I can't even imagine...

MAGI: They've been together nine.

AMAH: She still moving?

MAGI: So she say...asked me to pick up some boxes.

AMAH: *(Quietly.)* Rumour has it he's getting married.

MAGI: So soon. He hasn't told her anything. He still hasn't even moved his stuff yet.

AMAH: And she sacrificed so much. Gave up her share of the trust from her mother's life insurance to send him through school.

MAGI: No!

AMAH: So when it's her turn to go... All those years.

MAGI: And those babies.

AMAH: Yeh, thank god they didn't have any babies.

MAGI: No, no... Twice...

AMAH: No!

MAGI: First time, he told her he believed in a woman's right
to choose, but he didn't think that the relationship
was ready for—

AMAH: We didn't—

MAGI: Nobody did. Second time she miscarried.

AMAH: When? I don't—

MAGI: 'Bout the same time he left—no, it was before that.
She was by herself... Set down in a pool of blood.
She put it in a ziplock bag...in the freezer...all
purple and blue...

AMAH: Oohh God... No... Really?

MAGI: Yeh.

AMAH: Nooo... For real. I'm serious...

MAGI: Yeh!

AMAH: Show me.

          *(MAGI turns toward the living area and heads for the
          kitchen; AMAH follows closely behind. They approach
          the fridge and MAGI is about to open the freezer door
          when BILLIE enters from the bedroom. AMAH and
          MAGI stop abruptly, as if caught in the act.)*

AMAH: Billie!

MAGI: *(Overlapping.)* Hey girl!

          *(BILLIE waves to them as she exits into the
          bathroom. MAGI turns to AMAH.)*

          Or maybe I lied. Gotcha!

AMAH: You... You... little heifer—

          (MAGI laughs. AMAH gets infected and joins her.)

Scene 2

(Harlem, 1860: late summer — twilight. The instruments sing a blues from deep in the Mississippi delta, while a mature northern American voice reads from the Declaration of Independence. HIM steeps hot metal into cool water. He places the shackles on an anvil and hammers the metal into shape. HER is making repairs to a shawl with a needle.)

HER: I pray Cleotis is in heaven.

HIM: Yeh...I...um...I...

HER: You think Cleotis went to heaven?

HIM: Well, I... I don't...

HER: You think he's in hell?

HIM: No. No.

HER: Probably somewhere in between, though. Not Hades. Not God's kingdom. He's probably right there in the hardware store. Probably right there watching every time that Mr. Howard proudly hoists the mason jar. Every time they pay their penny to see through the formaldehyde. Cleotis is probably right there watching them gawk at his shriveled, pickled penis... You seen it?

HIM: No.

HER: You know who did the cutting, though?

HIM: No... Oh no...

HER: In France they got the vagina of a sister entombed for scientific research.

HIM: No!

HER: Venus, the Hottentot Venus. I read it in one of Miss Dessy's books. Saartjie—that's her real name, Saartjie Baartman. When Saartjie was alive they paraded her naked on a pay per view basis. Her derrière was amply endowed. People paid to see how big her butt was, and when she died, how big her pussy was.

HIM: Wooo!

HER: Human beings went and oohed and ahhed and paid money to see an endowment the creator bestowed on all of us.

HIM: That's...that's...so...so...

HER: They probably go to a special place though— Cleotis and Venus, Emmett. Purgatory. Venus and Cleotis fall in love, marry, but have no tools to consummate it. Must be a lot of us there walking around in purgatory without genitals.

(Beat.)

HIM: I've been meaning to...I want... *(Laughing to himself.)* I would like to...

HER: Yes...?

HIM: Talk. We should talk.

HER: Talk-talk?

HIM: Talk-talk.

HER: About what...? What's wrong?

HIM: Why must something be wrong —

HER: I... I just figured...figure...

(HIM takes HER's hand and kisses it, then places a white handkerchief into her palm.)

HIM: My heart...

(HIM closes HER's fingers around the handkerchief. He kisses her fingers. Opening her hand, she examines the cloth.)

HER: Little strawberries on a sheet of white. Berries in a field of snow... *(Sighing.)* Ah silk. It's beautiful.

HIM: It was my mother's. Given her by my father... from his mother before that. When she died she gave it me, insisting that when I found...chose...chose a wife...that I give it to her...to you heart.

HER: Oh... It is so beautiful.

HIM: There's magic in the web of it.

HER: So delicate...so old.

HIM: A token...an antique token of our ancient love.

HER: My ancient love...

HIM: My wife. My wife before I even met you. Let's do it. There's a war already brewing in the south. Canada freedom come.

HER: Yes?

HIM: Yes.

HER: We're really gonna go?

HIM: People will come to me and pay me for my work.

HER: Yes sir, Mr. Blacksmith, sir.

HIM: Can we have us a heap of children?

HER: Four boys and four girls.

HIM : And a big white house.

HER: A big house on an emerald hill.

HIM: Yeh...a white house, on an emerald hill, in Canada. *(Pause.)* I want to be with you 'till I'm too old to know. You know that.

HER: Even when my breasts fall to my toes?

HIM: I'll pick them up and carry them around for you.

HER: And when I can't remember my own name?

HIM: I'll call it out a thousand times a day.

HER: Then I'll think you're me.

HIM: I am you.

HER: And when I get old, and wrinkled, and enormously fat, you'll—

HIM: Fat? Naw. If you get fat, I'll have to leave your ass.

    (HIM kisses inside the crook of HER's arm.)

HER: Oh-oh. You're prospecting again.

HIM: I'm exploring the heightening Alleghenies of Pennsylvania.

    (HIM kisses HER.)

    The curvaceous slopes of California.

    (HIM kisses HER.)

    The red hills of Georgia, the mighty mountains of New York.

    (HIM kisses HER again.)

    I'm staking my claim

HER: I don't come cheap, you know.

HIM: I know…I'm offering more than money can buy.

HER: How much more?

HIM: This much.

    (HIM kisses HER.)

HER: I could buy that.

HIM: Could you buy this?

    (HIM kisses HER deeply.)

HER: Beloved…

    (HER kisses HIM.)

L-R: Nigel Shawn Williams, Alison Sealy-Smith

F-B: Alison Sealy-Smith, Dawn Roach

Scene 3

(Harlem, the present: late summer — morning. Strains of a melodious urban blues jazz keeps time with an oral address by Marcus Garvey on the need for African Americans to return to Africa.)

MAGI: No, I hate it.

AMAH: Come on. No one hates it.

MAGI: I do.

AMAH: Bah humbug?

MAGI: What?

AMAH: Scrooge?

MAGI: Oh no, no, no. You know what I hate about Christmas? Seven days to New Year's Eve. And I hate New Year's Eve. And you know what I really hate about New Year's Eve? It's not the being alone at midnight. It's not the being a wallflower at some bash, because you fired your escort, who asked for time and a half, after 10:00 p.m. It's not even because you babysat your friend's kids the previous two. I really hate New Year's Eve, because it's six weeks to Valentines Day. And what I really really hate about Valentines Day—well, maybe that's too strong. No. I really hate it. What I really hate about Valentines Day is…it's my birthday. Don't get me wrong, now. I'm glad I was born. But I look at my life—I'm more than halfway through it, and I wonder, what do I have to show for it? Anyway…

AMAH: Well you come and spend Kwanzaa with us this year.

MAGI: I don't know about the seven days, girl? Look,

I gotta go. I'm seeing a certain minister about a certain wedding.

AMAH: Whose wedding?

MAGI: Mine. And don't say a thing—you know, about him getting married, or anything.

(MAGI indicates the refrigerator.)

AMAH: Sealed.

MAGI: I'll drop by later.

AMAH: Alright.

MAGI: *(Shouting.)* Billie? I'm gonna drop by later with some boxes, OK?

BILLIE: *(Offstage.)* Thanks, Magi.

(MAGI exits. AMAH goes to the table and examines the small chemical factory.)

AMAH: Saracen's Compound... Woad... Hart's tongue... Prunella vulgaris...

(She picks up a book lying among the small packages and vials.)

Egyptian Alchemy: A Chemical Encyclopedia...

(She puts the book back in its place and picks up another vial.)

Nux Vomica, warning: Extremely poisonous. Can be ingested on contact with skin...

(AMAH quickly replaces the vial, wiping her hand on her clothes. She turns her attention to the kitchen. She cautiously approaches the refrigerator, and is about to open the freezer section when BILLIE comes out of the bathroom.)

BILLIE: Hey Amah.

AMAH: Oh—hi girl, how you feeling?

BILLIE: Thanks for making the house call, Amah.

AMAH: Child, you look so thin.

BILLIE: Well, I'm trying to lose a little baby fat before I die.

AMAH: Coffee?

BILLIE: Oh... Thanks. *(Pours coffee.)* You didn't have to come. I'm fine you know.

AMAH: You're very welcome. Come sit down.

> *(AMAH hands her the cup.)*

BILLIE: I didn't mean... Thank you.

AMAH: You washed your hair?

BILLIE: Yesterday.

AMAH: Good. A package came for you this morning.

BILLIE: Where?

AMAH: I put it beside the chemistry set. What is all that?

BILLIE: Don't touch anything!

AMAH: Alright—alright. I—

BILLIE: No. No. I—I mean, some of this stuff can be deadly unless mixed...or...or diluted. Some ancient Egyptian rejuvenation tonic. If it don't kill me, it'll make me brand new—or so it says. How's my baby?

AMAH: Jenny's fine. Andrew's taking her to her first African dance class today. You should see her in the little leotard...

BILLIE: I should be there.

AMAH: She's dying to come over for sausages and mashed potatoes.

BILLIE: Yeh, yes, soon. Real soon.

> *(AMAH prepares to twist BILLIE's hair. She opens a jar of hair oil and takes a generous portion of the oil, rubs it onto her hands and gently works it into BILLIE's hair.)*

AMAH:	She was so cute, today—you know what she did? She overheard me talking to Andrew about you, and I was saying I thought your breakdown was—
BILLIE:	You told her I had a nervous breakdown?
AMAH:	Oh— No. No. She overheard me—
BILLIE:	I am not having a nervous breakdown.
AMAH:	She didn't really understand. She thinks you've broken your legs and can't walk, you can't dance. She thinks you've broken your throat, and that's why she can't talk to you on the phone, that's why you don't sing to her on the phone anymore.
BILLIE:	Please don't tell her I'm crazy.
AMAH:	I never said you were crazy.
BILLIE:	I've just been…tired. Exhausted. I… I didn't want her to see this in me. She'd feel it in me. I never want her to feel this…
AMAH:	I know.
BILLIE:	But I'm fine now. Really, I'll be fine. I registered for school, I'm only taking one course this term, but that's cool. And first thing next week, I'm redoing the business plan for the salon.
AMAH:	You need to give me some of that tonic too, girl. That's the best kind of revenge, you know—living the good life.
BILLIE:	I thought I was living that life.
AMAH:	Maybe you were just dreaming.
	(AMAH takes a new lock of BILLIE's hair. Taking a large dab of oil, she applies it to the lock, rubbing the strand between her palms.)
BILLIE:	Remember when we moved in? The day Nelson and Winnie came to Harlem, remember? Winnie and Nelson—our welcoming committee. They'd blocked off the whole of 125th—it took us 45 minutes to convince the cops to let us through.

And me and you and Othe and Drew went down to hear them speak. And Drew went off in search of some grits from a street vendor. And you asked me to hold baby Jenny while you went to the restroom, when this man came up to us and took our picture. Asked to take our picture. Jenny in my arms. Othello beside me. "The perfect Black family". That's what he called us. "The perfect Black family".

(The phone rings.)

AMAH: I'll get it.

BILLIE: No. Let it ring. I know who it is. I can still feel him—feel when he's thinking of me. We've spoken... Must be three times, in the last two months. Something about $500 on my portion of his American Express card, which they'd cancel if I didn't pay the bill. Seems I did me some consumer therapy. Last time he called—mad—to announce that the card had been cancelled by AMEX, and that he hoped that I was pleased.

           (Beat.)

           And I was. Is that crazy?

AMAH: Don't sound crazy. Hold the hair oil for me.

BILLIE: I used to pray that he was calling to say he's sorry. To say how he'd discovered a deep confusion in himself. But now...

           (The phone stops ringing.)

           I have nothing to say to him. What could I say? Othello, how is the fairer sexed one you love to dangle from your arm the one you love for herself and preferred to the deeper sexed one is she softer does she smell of tea roses and baby powder does she sweat white musk from between her toes do her thighs touch I am not curious just want to know do her breasts fill the cup of your hand the lips of your tongue not too dark you like a little milk with your nipple don't you no I'm not curious just want to know.

AMAH: You tell Jenny colour's only skin deep.

BILLIE: The skin holds everything in. It's the largest organ
                 in the human body. Slash the skin by my belly and
                 my intestines fall out.

AMAH: Hold the hair oil up.

                 (AMAH takes a dab of oil from the jar.)

BILLIE :   I thought I saw them once, you know—on the
                 subway. I had to renew my prescription. And I
                 spot them—him and her. My chest is pounding.
                 My legs can't move. From the back, I see the sharp
                 barber's line, separating his tightly coiled hair
                 from the nape of the skin at the back of his neck.
                 His skin is soft there…and I have to kick away the
                 memory nudging its way into my brain. My lips
                 on his neck, gently…holding him… Here, before
                 me—his woman—all blonde hair and blonde legs.
                 Her weight against his chest. His arm around her
                 shoulders, his thumb resting on the gold of her
                 hair. He's proud. You can see he's proud. He isn't
                 just any Negro. He's special. That's why she's with
                 him. And she…she…she flaunts. Yes, she flaunts.
                 They are before. I am behind, stuck there on the
                 platform. My tongue is pushing hard against the
                 roof of my mouth…trying to hold up my brain,
                 or something. 'Cause my brain threatens to fall.
                 Fall down through the roof of my mouth, and be
                 swallowed up. Slowly, slowly, I press forward,
                 toward them. I'm not aiming for them though. I'm
                 aiming with them in mind. I'm aiming for beyond
                 the yellow line, into the tracks. The tunnel all three
                 of us will fall into can be no worse than the one I'm
                 trapped in now. I walk—no, well hover really. I'm
                 walking on air. I feel sure of myself for the first time
                 in weeks. Only to be cut off by a tall grey man in a
                 grey uniform, who isn't looking where he's going,
                 or maybe I'm not— Maybe he knew my aim. He
                 looks at me. I think he looks at me. He brushes past.
                 Then a sound emanating from…from…from my
                 uterus, slips out of my mouth, shatters the spell.
                 They turn their heads—the couple. They see me. It
                 isn't even him.

(The phone rings again.)

AMAH: It could be your father, you know. He's been trying to get in touch with you. Says he doesn't know if you're dead or alive. He was calling Drew even up to this morning.

BILLIE: My father...I wouldn't have anything to say. It's been so long. What would I say?

(The phone stops ringing.)

AMAH: He's been in the hospital, you know. Something about his liver.

BILLIE: He hauled us all the way back to Nova Scotia from the Bronx, to be near Granma, when Mama died.

AMAH: I love that Nova Scotia was a haven for slaves way before the underground railroad. I love that...

BILLIE: He's a sot. That's academia speak for alcoholic. My Dad, the drunk of Dartmouth.

AMAH: You're still his children.

BILLIE: A detail I'm glad he's recalled.

AMAH: Better late than never.

BILLIE: Too little, too late.

AMAH: Forgiveness is a virtue.

BILLIE: What?

AMAH: Forgiveness is a virtue.

BILLIE: Girl, patience is a virtue.

AMAH: Well......forgiveness is up there...

BILLIE: Did Drew tell you about the time my father sang to me at my high school graduation dinner?

AMAH: Nooo. That's lovely. My father never sang to me at my graduation.

BILLIE: We were eating. He was standing on top of the banquet table.

AMAH:	Nooo!
BILLIE:	It's the truth!

(Pause.)

AMAH:	Can I get a glass of water?
BILLIE:	Yeh. Yeh, help yourself.

(AMAH goes into the kitchen.)

I've got O.J. in the fridge, if you want.

AMAH: Water will do, thanks. Do you have any…ice in your freezer?

BILLIE: I'll get it.

AMAH: I can get it.

(BILLIE gets up quickly, and heads toward the kitchen.)

BILLIE: It's OK. It's OK. I'll get it for you.

(BILLIE opens the freezer and gets her the ice, closing the freezer door immediately behind her.)

AMAH: Thanks. *(Beat.)* What's in there?

BILLIE: Frozen shit.

(The phone begins to ring again. Both women look toward it.)

Scene 4

(Same day: noontime. Accompanying the sound of rushing water and the polyrhythmic chorus of strings, Martin Luther King continues to assert his dream, its relationship to the American Constitution, and the Declaration of Independence.)

OTHELLO: *(Offstage.)* Billie!

(Silence. He knocks again.)

Billie?! *(To MONA.)* I don't think she's there.

(OTHELLO unlocks the door. He enters. We recognize him as the man in both 1860 and 1928.)

Billie? Mona and I are here to pick up the rest of my things. Billie?

(He hears the shower. He goes over to the bathroom door. He knocks.)

Billie?...

(BILLIE screams. We hear something crash.)

It's just me...I tried to call. You should get that machine fixed.

BILLIE: *(Offstage.)* I'll be out in a minute.

(OTHELLO returns to MONA at the entrance. We see nothing of her but brief glimpses of a bare arm and a waft of light brown hair.)

OTHELLO: It's OK Mona, she's in there. Why don't you wait in the car.

MONA: *(Offstage.)* She'll have to get used to me sometime.

OTHELLO: I'll be down in a flash. It won't take me that long.

(She doesn't answer.)

Hey, hey, hey!

MONA: *(Offstage.)* Hey yourself. I do have other things to take care of, you know.

(He kisses her.)

OK…I still haven't found anything blue. I'll scour the stores. I'll be back in a couple of hours.

OTHELLO: Alright.

MONA: *(Offstage.)* Alright.

(He brings in several large empty boxes. He closes the door and looks around. He sees a burning cigarette, picks it up, looks at it, then puts it out. He takes off his jacket. Then he takes several albums from a shelf and places them on the floor. He begins to form two piles. He picks up one of the albums and begins to laugh. BILLIE enters dressed in a robe.)

BILLIE: What are you doing here?

OTHELLO: I came over to pack my things. The movers are coming in the morning. I tried to call…

BILLIE: You took my pot.

OTHELLO: What…

BILLIE: My pot. The cast iron Dutch pot.

OTHELLO: Oh… Well, you never use it.

BILLIE: I want it back.

OTHELLO: You never use it.

BILLIE: The one with the yellow handle.

OTHELLO: We need it to make gumbo.

BILLIE: She uses it?

OTHELLO: I need it to make gumbo.

BILLIE: She needs my pot? The one with the carrying rings.

OTHELLO: It was a gift to both of us.

BILLIE: From my father.

OTHELLO: I'll bring it back tomorrow.

BILLIE: If you don't have it here for me inside of 30 minutes, I will break every jazz recording on that shelf.

OTHELLO: You want me to go all the way back for something you don't even use.

BILLIE: Let me see…

OTHELLO: You never used it.

BILLIE: Abbey Lincoln…

> *(She takes the album from the table. Takes the record from the jacket and breaks it in two. She reaches for another album. OTHELLO picks up the broken record.)*

Aah. Max Roach.

> *(She takes the cover off the Max Roach album.)*

OTHELLO: The Abbey Lincoln was yours.

> *(She breaks the Max Roach record too.)*

OK. OK, I'll go and get it.

> *(He picks up his jacket and proceeds to the door.)*

BILLIE: Fine. It's fine.

OTHELLO: Excuse me?

BILLIE: It's fine. Tomorrow's fine.

> *(Pause. He turns toward her.)*

OTHELLO: OK.

(Pause. He puts his jacket down again. Pause.)

How are you? You look well.

BILLIE: I'm fine. And you?

OTHELLO: Great... Good.

(Pause.)

BILLIE: Well you know where your stuff is.

OTHELLO: Yep... Yes.

(Pause.)

BILLIE: Drink?

OTHELLO: What?

BILLIE: Would you like something to drink?

OTHELLO: Sure... Yes.. What do you—

BILLIE: Peppermint, fennel, chamomile... No... Just peppermint and fennel. Coffee, wine, cognac, water.

OTHELLO: What are you having?

BILLIE: Cognac.

OTHELLO: Oh. Well... That'll do.

(BILLIE goes to the kitchen.)

Where's my suitcase?

BILLIE: Where you left it.

(Pause.)

OTHELLO: So you're staying on then?

BILLIE: No.

OTHELLO: Where are you... You know... I mean, things are tight, money-wise, but I'll still put money in your account... When I can... I mean, I hope we can keep in touch.

(She hands him a glass of cognac.)

Thank you.

BILLIE: You're welcome.

(Pause.)

OTHELLO: You've lost weight. You look great. *(He takes a large gulp.)* Aaahh! Yes!

> *(OTHELLO looks at BILLIE for a moment. He then takes one of the boxes and places it at his feet. He approaches the bookshelf. He takes down a large book.)*

African Mythology… Is this mine or yours?

BILLIE: Mine…I think… I don't know.

OTHELLO: This is going to be interesting.

BILLIE: Take what you like. I don't care.

> *(OTHELLO takes another book.)*

OTHELLO: *The Great Chain of Being?*

BILLIE: From man to mollusk. The scientific foundation for why we're not human. An African can't really be a woman, you know. My department agreed to let me take only one course this year—I'm taking a reading course.

OTHELLO: Yours… Yours… Mine… *Black Psychology,* you keeping this?

BILLIE: Yeh. *(She takes the books from him.)* You'd think there was more information on Black people and mental health. You know… Christ, we've been here, what, 400 years. No money in it I guess…

OTHELLO: What's money got to do with it?

BILLIE: You know, grants… Scholarships…

OTHELLO: Race is not an obscure idea.

> *(He places several books into a box.)*

BILLIE: In genetics, or the study of what's wrong with people of African descent—The Heritage Foundation will give you tons of dough to prove the innate inferiority of... The Shakespeare's mine, but you can have it.

OTHELLO: Sure, if you don't—

BILLIE: No. The Heritage Foundation—that's where that guy Murray, et al, got most of their money for Bell Curve—I think... There's just no-one out there willing to give you a scholarship to prove that we're all mad.

OTHELLO: We're all mad. This is the founding principle of your thesis?

BILLIE: Well, not mad... I mean... Well... Psychologically dysfunctional, then. All cultural groups are to some degree ethnocentric: We—they. But not all inter-cultural relations are of an inferior/superior type.

OTHELLO: Thus we're not all mad.

(He returns to the bookshelf.)

BILLIE: No, no. In America, this race shit is classic behavioural disorder. Obsessions. Phobias. Delusions. Notions of persecution. Delusions of grandeur. Any one or combination of these can produce behaviours which categorize oneself as superior and another as inferior. You see, this kind of dysfunction is systemically supported by the larger society. Psychology only sees clients who can no longer function in society. We're all mad. We just appear to be functional.

OTHELLO: And your solution?

BILLIE: You'll have to buy my book.

(Pause. They continue packing.)

How's the teaching?

OTHELLO: Fine... Great...

BILLIE: Good.

(*Pause.*)

OTHELLO: I'll be heading the department's courses in Cyprus next summer.

BILLIE: I thought you told me Christopher…What's his name?

OTHELLO: Chris Yago?

BILLIE: Yeh, Yago.

OTHELLO: Well everyone thought he would get it. I thought he'd get it. So a whole bunch of them are challenging affirmative action.

BILLIE: Rednecks in academia.

OTHELLO: No, no… Well….. I think it's a good thing.

BILLIE: Pul-eese.

OTHELLO: Using discrimination to cure discrimination is not—

BILLIE: We're talking put asides of 5%. 5% of everything available to Whites. They've still got 95.

OTHELLO: Billie… Injustice against Blacks can't be cured by injustice against Whites…you know that.

BILLIE: And younger people won't have the same opportunities you had.

OTHELLO: Now look who's sounding White.

BILLIE: Who said you sounded White?

OTHELLO: It's implied… No-one at school tells me I don't know how to do my job…it's implied. I'll be at a faculty meeting, I'll make a suggestion and it'll be ignored. Not five minutes later, someone else will make the exact same suggestion and everyone will agree to it. Mona noticed it too. They think I'm only there because I'm Black. I've tested it.

BILLIE: So let me get this straight, you're against affirmative action in order for White people to respect you.

OTHELLO:	For my peers......my peers to respect me. You know what it's like. Every day I have to prove to them that I can do my job. I feel that any error I make only goes to prove them right.
BILLIE:	Well you must be perfect. Mona respects you.
OTHELLO:	Well, she really sees me. She was the only other faculty to support me on the MLK Day assembly. When we played the video—
BILLIE:	The 'I have a dream' speech?
OTHELLO:	They understood. For a moment I got them to understand.

(He picks up several books and places them in a box.)

BILLIE:	"America has defaulted on this promissory note insofar as her...
OTHELLO & BILLIE:	...citizens of colour are concerned.
OTHELLO:	Instead of honoring this sacred obligation, America has given its coloured people a...
OTHELLO & BILLIE:	bad cheque...
BILLIE:	...a cheque that has come back marked...
OTHELLO & BILLIE:	...'insufficient funds'."
BILLIE:	The man was a... a...
OTHELLO:	Poet... Visionary.
BILLIE:	A prophet.
OTHELLO:	After all he'd been through in his life, he could still see that at a deeper level we're all the same.

(Pause.)

BILLIE:	I'm not the same.
OTHELLO:	In the eyes of God, Billie, we're all the same.

BILLIE: One day little Black boys and little White girls—

OTHELLO: You're delusional.

BILLIE: You're the one looking for White respect.

OTHELLO: Wrong again! White respect, Black respect, it's all the same to me.

BILLIE: Right on brother man!

OTHELLO: When I was growing up.....in a time of Black pride—it was something to say you were Black. Before that, I'd say... My family would say we're Cuban... It takes a long time to work through some of those things. I am a member of the human race.

BILLIE: Oh, that's a switch. What happened to all that J. A. Rogers stuff you were pushing. Blacks created the world, Blacks are the progenitors of European civilization, gloriana... Constantly trying to prove you're as good, no, better than White people. White people are always the line for you, aren't they? The rule...the margin...the variable of control. We are Black. Whatever we do is Black.

OTHELLO: I'm so tired of this race shit, Billie. There are alternatives—

BILLIE: Like what? Oh yes, White.

OTHELLO: Oh, don't be so—

BILLIE: Isn't that really what not acting Black, or feeling Black means.

OTHELLO: Liberation has no colour.

BILLIE: But progress is going to White schools...proving we're as good as Whites...like some holy grail...all that we're taught in those White schools. All that is in us. Our success is Whiteness. We religiously seek to have what they have. Access to the White man's world. The White man's job.

OTHELLO: That's economics.

BILLIE: White economics.

OTHELLO: God! Black women always—

BILLIE: No. Don't even go there…

OTHELLO: I… You… Forget it!

BILLIE: (*Quietly at first.*) Yes, you can forget it, can't you.
             I don't have that…that luxury. When I go into a
             store, I always know when I'm being watched. I can
             feel it. They want to see if I'm gonna slip some of
             their stuff into my pockets. When someone doesn't
             serve me, I think it's because I'm Black. When a
             clerk won't put the change into my held-out hand,
             I think it's because I'm Black. When I hear about a
             crime, any crime, I pray to God the person who they
             think did it isn't Black. I'm even suspicious of the
             word Black. Who called us Black anyway? It's not
             a country, it's not a racial category, its not even the
             colour of my skin. And don't give me this content
             of one's character B.S. I'm sorry…I am sorry…I
             had a dream. A dream that one day a Black man
             and a Black woman might find… Where jumping a
             broom was a solemn eternal vow that… I… Let's…
             Can we just get this over with?

             (*She goes to the window.*

             Silence.

             He moves toward her.)

OTHELLO: I know…I know. I'm sorry…

BILLIE: Yeh…

OTHELLO: I care…you know that.

BILLIE: I know.

             (*Silence.*)

OTHELLO: I never thought I'd miss Harlem.

             (*Pause.*)

BILLIE: You still think it's a reservation?

OTHELLO: Homeland / reservation.

BILLIE: A sea of Black faces.

OTHELLO: Africatown, USA.

(Pause.)

BILLIE: When we lived in the Village, sometimes, I'd be on the subway and I'd miss my stop. And I'd just sit there, past midtown, past the upper west side, and somehow I'd end up here. And I'd just walk. I love seeing all these brown faces.

OTHELLO: Yeh...

BILLIE: Since they knocked down the old projects, I can see the Schomberg Museum from here. You still can't make out Harlem Hospital. I love that I can see the Apollo from our—from my balcony.

OTHELLO: Fire escape.

BILLIE: Patio.

OTHELLO: You never did find a pair of lawn chairs, and a table to fit in that space.

BILLIE: Terrace.

OTHELLO: I never saw the beauty in it.

BILLIE: Deck. My deck.

OTHELLO: I wish...

(He looks at her.)

BILLIE: That old building across the street? I didn't know this, but that used to be the Hotel Theresa. That's where Castro stayed when he came to New York... Must have been the fifties. Ron Brown's father used to run that hotel.

OTHELLO: I...... I...... I miss you so much sometimes. Nine years...it's a long time.

BILLIE: I know.

OTHELLO: I'm really not trying to hurt you, Billie.

BILLIE: I know.

OTHELLO: I never meant to hurt you.

              (He strokes her face.)

BILLIE: I know.

OTHELLO: God you're so beautiful.

              (He kisses her. She does not resist.)

BILLIE: I....don't.... I feel…

              (He kisses her again.)

BILLIE: What are you doing?

OTHELLO: I…I'm…I'm exploring the heightening Alleghenies of Pennsylvania.

              (He kisses her again.)

              The curvaceous slopes of California.

              (He kisses her again.)

              The red hills of Georgia, the mighty mountains of New York. Such sad eyes.

              (He kisses her again.)

              I'm an equal opportunity employer.

              (Pause.)

              I am an equal opportunity employer.

              (Pause.)

              I say, I'm an equal opportunity employer, then you say, I don't come…

BILLIE: I don't come cheap, you know.

OTHELLO: I'm offering more than money can buy.

BILLIE: How much more?

OTHELLO: This much.

          (He kisses her.)

BILLIE: I could buy that.

OTHELLO: Could you buy this?

          (He kisses her deeply.)

BILLIE: Be... Be... Beloved.

          (She kisses him.)

Scene 5

(Same day: early afternoon. The stringed duet croons gently as Malcolm X speaks about the need for Blacks to turn their gaze away from Whiteness so that they can see each other with new eyes. OTHELLO is lying in the bed. BILLIE is in the living room, smoking a cigarette.)

OTHELLO: I've missed you.

BILLIE: That's nice.

OTHELLO: By the looks of things, I miss you even now.

BILLIE: I'm coming.

OTHELLO: I noticed.

BILLIE: Sometimes… Sometimes when we make love. Sometimes every moment lines up into one moment. And I'm holding you. And I can't tell where I end, or you begin. I see everything. All my ancestors lined up below me......like a Makonde statue, or something. It's like… I know. I know I'm supposed to be here. Everything is here.

OTHELLO: Sounds crowded to me.

BILLIE: It's actually quite empty.

OTHELLO: Not as empty as this bed is feeling right about now.

BILLIE: I'm coming. I'm coming.

(She hurriedly stubs the cigarette out, and heads toward the bedroom. The apartment buzzer rings. BILLIE goes to the intercom.)

BILLIE: Hi Magi. I…er…I'm kinda busy right now.

MONA: *(Through intercom.)* It's Mona. Could I have a word with Othello.

OTHELLO: *(Overlapping.)* Shit!

BILLIE: One second please.

> *(He rushes to the intercom, while attempting to put his clothes back on. BILLIE tries to hold back her laughter. Her laughter begins to infect OTHELLO. He puts a finger over his mouth indicating to BILLIE to be quiet.)*

OTHELLO: Hey Mone... Mone, I'm not done yet. There's more here than I imagined. Why don't I call you when I'm done.

> *(MONA does not respond. OTHELLO's demeanour changes.)*

Mone? Mona? I'm coming, OK? I'll be right... Just wait there one second, OK? OK?

> *(BILLIE is unable to hide her astonishment.)*

MONA: *(Through intercom.)* OK.

OTHELLO: OK.

> *(He steps away from the intercom to finish putting on his clothes. BILLIE stares at him.)*

I'll be back in... Uh... I just have to go straighten... Uh... She wants to help...help pack. You'll have to get used to her sometime. I mean... I...

> *(BILLIE continues to stare steadily at OTHELLO as he struggles with the buttons on his shirt.)*

I'm sorry... Well...... I'll be right... I'll be back.

> *(He exits. BILLIE does not move.)*

Scene 6

(Harlem, 1860: late summer—night. A whining delta blues slides and blurs while the deeply resonant voice of Paul Robeson talks of his forbears, whose blood is in the American soil. HIM is hammering a newly-forged horseshoe, HER rushes in holding a large carrying bag.)

HER:

Oh...let me catch—catch my breath... I thought I was seen...Oh my... I...I've packed a change of clothes for both of us, some loaves... I liberated the leftover bacon from yesterday's meal, from out the pantry, seeing how it was staring me right in the face when I was cleaning. It won't be missed. I wish I could pack old Betsy in my bag. She'd be sure an' give us some good fresh milk each mornin'. Oh—and I packed a fleece blanket. I hear the nights get good and cold further north you go. And... did I forget...no... Nothing forgotten. Oh yes, I borrowed the big carving knife—for the bacon, a' course. You still working on those shoes for Miss Dessy's stallion... Let her send it to town, or get some other slave to do that... She's going to be mad as hell you took off in any event... May as well not finish the shoes, it won't placate her none...

(HIM picks up the horseshoe with a pair of tongs. HIM inspects it carefully. HIM puts the shoe to one side and retrieves the shackles. HIM takes a chamois and begins to polish the metal.)

(Pause.) O? O? Othello? The moon'll be rising. We've got to make any headway under cover of dark ... Othello, why you trying to please her. I'm so tired of pleasing her. I'm so tired of pleasing White folks. Up in Canada, we won't have to please no White folks no how. I hear they got

sailing ships leaving for Africa every day. Canada freedom come... O? Othello? Are you coming?

HIM: I can't.

HER: If we make it to the border there's people there'll help us wade that water—help us cross over.

HIM: I'm not going.

HER: A big white house on an emerald hill...

HIM: I know.

HER: You need more time, O? I can wait for you. Finish her shoes, I'll... I can wait—

HIM : No. No.

(Pause.)

HER: You love her.

HIM: Her father going to war.

HER: You love her?

HIM: I love you. It's just... She needs me. She respects me. Looks up to me, even. I love you. It's just... When I'm with her I feel like...a man. I want...I need to do for her...

HER: Do you love her?

HIM: Yes.

HER: Fight with me......I would fight with you. Suffer with me, O... I would suffer with you...

(Silence.)

Scene 7

(Harlem, present: late summer—late afternoon. Dulcet blue tones barely swing as Louis Farrakhan waxes eloquent on African Americans being caught in the gravity of American society.)

MAGI: And you know what he says, after turning on the baseball game, in the middle of my romantic dinner? Eyes glued to the screen, he says, I bet you've never made love to a man with 26-inch biceps!

BILLIE: *(Smiles.)* Oh…no…

MAGI: I'm telling you, girl. Macho Mack, spot him at any locale selling six-packs. Easily recognizable, everything about him is permanently flexed. His favourite pastime? Weekend NFL football, Monday night football, USFL football—even Canadian foot… You look like you're feeling better. Amah did a great job with your hair.

BILLIE: What's her motto? We lock heads and minds.

MAGI: Hey, can I borrow that beautiful African boubou—I got me a date with an African prince. The brother has it going on! Oh…you already have boxes.

(BILLIE begins placing some of the wrapped objects into a box.)

BILLIE: They're his box—

MAGI: When… He came over?

BILLIE: I even spoke to her.

MAGI: You saw her?

BILLIE: No. Want this mask?

MAGI:	You met her?
BILLIE:	No. Want this mask?.
MAGI:	I'll keep it for you —
BILLIE:	I...er.......I don't know how long these things will have to stay in storage.
MAGI:	You don't have to move, you know. It's not rented yet. I mean, I can always lower the—
BILLIE:	No, no... I'm moving on.
MAGI:	Good. Good. To where? Where are you going? You haven't given me a date or anything. I've got bills to pay too, you know. When d'you plan to leave? Where are you going?
BILLIE:	I might go......stay with Jenny. I could go home.
MAGI:	I'll keep it for you —
BILLIE:	I don't want anything that's—that was ours. If you don't want it, that's OK, I'll just trash it.

> (BILLIE throws the mask onto the floor. It breaks into several pieces.)

MAGI:	Something happened. What happened?
BILLIE:	Nothing.
MAGI:	Did he tell you about... What did he say to you?
BILLIE:	I'm just tired. Tired of sleeping. Tired of night. It lays over me like a ton of white feathers. Swallows me up. The movers are coming in the morning to pick up his things. It's OK. I'm fine. You know... I've lived all my life believing in lies.
MAGI:	Well, getting your Masters isn't a lie.
BILLIE:	It's about proving, isn't it? Proving I'm as good as... I'm as intelligent as...
MAGI:	Nothing wrong with that.
BILLIE:	I don't want anything... Believe in anything. Really.

I've gotta get out of here. I don't even believe in Harlem anymore.

MAGI: Come on…

BILLIE: It's all an illusion. All some imagined idealistic… I dunno.

MAGI: When I go out my door, I see all the beauty of my Blackness reflected in the world around me.

BILLIE: Yeh, and all my wretchedness by the time I get to the end of the block.

MAGI: Billie, he's the one who wants to White wash his life.

BILLIE: Corporeal malediction.

MAGI: Corp-o-re-all mal-e… Oooh that's good.

BILLIE: A Black man afflicted with Negrophobia.

MAGI: Girl, you on a roll now!

BILLIE: No, no. A crumbled racial epidermal schema…

MAGI: Who said school ain't doing you no good.

BILLIE: …causing predilections to coitus denegrification.

MAGI: Booker T. Uppermiddleclass III. He can be found in predominantly White neighborhoods. He refers to other Blacks as "them". His greatest accomplishment was being invited to the White House by George Bush to discuss the "Negro problem."

BILLIE: Now, that is frightening.

MAGI: No, what's frightening is the fact that I dated him.

BILLIE: What does it say… about us?

MAGI: Who?

BILLIE: You and me.

MAGI: Girl, I don't know. I can't even want to go there.

BILLIE: Ohh... Oh well... Least he's happy though. What does he say? Now he won't have to worry that a White woman will emotionally mistake him for the father that abandoned her.

MAGI: Isn't he worried the White woman might mistake him for the butler?

BILLIE: He'd be oh so happy to oblige.

MAGI: I see them do things for White women they wouldn't dream of doing for me.

BILLIE: It is a disease. We get infected as children, and... and the bacteria... the virus slowly spreads, disabling the entire system.

MAGI: Are we infected too?

(There is knocking at the apartment door.)

Speaking of White minds parading around inside of Black bodies—you want me to stay?

BILLIE: Don't you have a date?

MAGI: Hakim. But I can cancel...

There is knocking at the door again.

BILLIE: I'm OK. I'm OK. I'm fine... Truly.

(BILLIE opens the door. OTHELLO enters.)

OTHELLO: The pot!

(He hands the pot to BILLIE.)

Magi!

MAGI: How's Harlumbia?

OTHELLO: Columbia?

MAGI: Harlumbia—those 10 square blocks of Whitedom, owned by Columbia University, set smack dab in the middle of Harlem.

OTHELLO: Harlumbia, as you call it, is dull without you.

MAGI:　　　You could steal honey from a bee, couldn't you. Better watch you don't get stung. Well, I'm off to doll myself up. Billie…

BILLIE:　　Yeh, I'll get that boubou…

(BILLIE goes into the bedroom. After a few moments of silence.)

MAGI:　　　Why haven't you told her yet?

OTHELLO:　About?—Oh yes… Yeh… I wanted to…

(BILLIE returns with a beautiful multicoloured boubou.)

BILLIE:　　He won't be able to resist you…

MAGI:　　　Thank you, thank you. Later you two.

OTHELLO:　I'll be in touch…

BILLIE:　　I'm keeping my fingers crossed for you.

MAGI:　　　Good, I'm running out of time.

(MAGI exits. OTHELLO enters. BILLIE closes the door. There is a long awkward silence. BILLIE continues placing wrapped objects into her boxes. OTHELLO steps on a piece of the broken mask. He picks it up, looks at it, then places it on the mantel. He goes over to the bookshelf and begins to pack more of his possessions into his boxes.)

OTHELLO:　They're coming at nine.

BILLIE:　　Oh… Er… I'll be out of your way.

OTHELLO:　You can be here…

BILLIE:　　No. No. No. I have an appointment……an early appointment.

OTHELLO:　Either way…

(They continue packing.)

Ah… I've been meaning to tell you……things

are real.....money's real tight right now, what with buying the apartment, and moving and everything...I won't be able to cover your tuition this semester. I'll try and put money in your account when I can. Maybe—

BILLIE: I told you, I'm only taking one course. If you cover that, I won't be taking a full load 'till next—

OTHELLO: I know, that's what I'm saying.... I can't... I just can't do it right now.

BILLIE: It's one course...

OTHELLO: It's $5000.

BILLIE: You promised...

OTHELLO: I'm mortgaged up the wazoo. I don't have it. I just don't have $5000, right now.

BILLIE: Ooh.....okay.

OTHELLO : I would if I could, you know that.

(He continues to pack.)

I think I brought the bookshelf with me when we first—

BILLIE: Take it all.

OTHELLO: I don't want all of it.

BILLIE: I'm keeping the bed.

OTHELLO: What about the rest...

BILLIE: If you don't want it... I'm giving it away...

OTHELLO: OK, if you're throwing it out...

BILLIE: I'm keeping the bed.

(They continue packing in silence.)

OTHELLO: We're getting married.

(Pause.)

Me and Mona. We're engaged... Officially.

(Very long pause.)

BILLIE: Congratulations.

OTHELLO: I wanted to tell you... Hear it from the horse's mouth... Hear it from me first. You know...

(Pause.)

BILLIE: Yeh... Yes. Yes. Congratulations.

OTHELLO: Mona wanted me to tell you.

BILLIE: Yes. Yes. Being a feminist and everything— A woman's right to know—since we're all in the struggle.... I thought you hated feminists.

OTHELLO: Well... I didn't mean that. I mean...the White women's movement is different.

BILLIE: Just Black feminists.

OTHELLO: No, no... White men have maintained a firm grasp of the pants. I mean, White men have economic and political pants that White women have been demanding to share.

BILLIE: White wisdom from the mouth of the mythical Negro.

OTHELLO: Don't you see! That's exactly my point! You... The Black feminist position as I experience it in this relationship, leaves me feeling unrecognized as a man. The message is, Black men are poor fathers, poor partners, or both. Black women wear the pants that Black men were prevented from wearing... I believe in tradition. You don't support me. Black women are more concerned with their careers than their husbands. There was a time when women felt satisfied, no, honoured being a balance to their spouse, at home, supporting the family, playing her role—

BILLIE: Which women? I mean, which women are you referring to? Your mother worked all her life. My mother worked, her mother worked… Most Black women have been working like mules since we arrived on this continent. Like mules. When White women were burning their bras, we were hired to hold their tits up. We looked after their homes, their children… I don't support you? My mother's death paid your tuition, not mine…

OTHELLO: Can't we even pretend to be civil? Can't we? I know this isn't easy. It's not easy for me either. Do you ever consider that?

BILLIE: You like it easy, don't you.

OTHELLO: The truth is, this is too fucking difficult.

BILLIE: You wouldn't know the truth if it stood up and knocked you sideways.

OTHELLO: You don't want the truth. You want me to tell you what you want to hear. No, no, you want to know the truth? I'll tell you the truth. Yes, I prefer White women. They are easier—before and after sex. They wanted me and I wanted them. They weren't filled with hostility about the unequal treatment they were getting at their jobs. We'd make love and I'd fall asleep not having to beware being mistaken for someone's inattentive father. I'd explain that I wasn't interested in a committed relationship right now, and not be confused with every lousy lover, or husband that had ever left them lying in a gutter of unresolved emotions. It's the truth. To a Black woman, I represent every Black man she has ever been with and with whom there was still so much to work out. The White women I loved saw me—could see me. Look, I'm not a junkie. I don't need more than one lover to prove my manhood. I have no children. I did not leave you, your mother, or your aunt, with six babies and a whole lotta love. I am a very single, very intelligent, very employed Black man. And with White women it's good. It's nice. Anyhow, we're all equal in the eyes of God, aren't we? Aren't we?

(BILLIE stares at OTHELLO. He continues to pack.)

Scene 8

(Harlem, 1928: late summer — night. The cello and bass moan, almost dirge-like, in harmonic tension to the sound of Jesse Jackson's oratory. SHE holds a straight-edged razor in her bloodied palms. HE lies on the floor in front of her, motionless, the handkerchief in his hand.)

SHE: Deadly deadly straw little strawberries it's so beautiful you kissed my fingers you pressed this cloth into my palm buried it there an antique token our ancient all these tiny red dots on a sheet of white my fingernails are white three hairs on my head are white the whites of my eyes are white too the palms of my hands and my feet are white you're all I'd ever and you my my I hate Sssshh. Shhhhh OK. OK. OK. I'm OK alright don't don't don't don't my eyes on the shadow sparrow my sense in my feet my hands my head shine the light there please scream no sing sing *(SHE tries to sing.)* and if I get a notion to jump into the ocean, ain't nobody's business if I do do do do If I go to church on Sunday then shimmy down on Monday t'ain't nobody's business if I...

Scene 9

(Harlem, present: late summer—early evening. The instruments sound out a deep cerulean blues, while Malcolm X almost scats the question, "What difference does colour make?" OTHELLO continues to pack. BILLIE sits on the floor by the bed watching him from the bedroom.)

OTHELLO: I didn't mean—what I said. You know that. I just... Sometimes you make me so mad I... People change, Billie. That's just human nature. Our experiences, our knowledge transforms us. That's why education is so powerful, so erotic. The transmission of words from mouth to ear. Her mouth to my ear. Knowledge. A desire for that distant thing I know nothing of, but yearn to hold for my very own. My Mama used to say, you have to be three times as good as a White child to get by, to do well. A piece of that pie is mine. I don't want to change the recipe. I am not minor. I am not a minority. I used to be a minority when I was a kid. I mean my culture is not my mother's culture—the culture of my ancestors. My culture is Wordsworth, Shaw, *Leave it to Beaver, Dirty Harry.* I drink the same water, read the same books. You're the problem if you don't see beyond my skin. If you don't hear my educated English, if you don't understand that I am a middle class educated man. I mean, what does Africa have to do with me. We struttin' around professing some imaginary connection for a land we don't know. Never seen. Never gonna see. We lie to ourselves saying, ah yeh, mother Africa, middle passage, suffering, the Whites did it to me, it's the White's fault. Strut around in African cloth pretending we human now. We human now. Some of us are beyond that now. Spiritually beyond this race shit bullshit now.

I am an American. The slaves were freed over 130 years ago. In 1967 it was illegal for a Black to marry a White in sixteen states. That was less than thirty years ago…in my lifetime. Things change, Billie. I am not my skin. My skin is not me.

Scene 10

(Harlem, same day: night. A rhapsody of sound keeps time with Christopher Darden as he asks O. J. Simpson to approach the jury and try on the bloody glove. The apartment is virtually full of boxes. BILLIE is by the chemical factory at the table. The book of Egyptian Alchemy sits open upon it. Something is boiling in the flask and steam is coming out of the condenser. With rubber gloved hands she adds several drops of a violet liquid into the flask. She picks up a large white handkerchief with pretty red strawberries embroidered on it.)

BILLIE: I have a plan, my love. My mate....throughout eternity. Feel what I feel. Break like I break. No more—no less. You'll judge me harsher. I know. While Susan Smith... She blamed some imaginary Black man for the murder of her two boys and that's why authorities didn't suspect her for nearly two weeks. Stopping every Black man with a burgundy sedan from Union, South Carolina, to the Oranges of New Jersey. And you're still wondering what made her do it. What was she going through to make her feel that this was her only way out. Yet I'll be discarded as some kind of unconscionable bitter shadow, or something. Ain't I a woman? This is my face you take for night—the biggest shadow in the world. I... I have nothing more to lose. Nothing. Othello? I am preparing something special for you... Othe... Othello. A gift for you, and your new bride. Once you gave me a handkerchief. An heirloom. This handkerchief, your mother's..... given by your father. From his mother before that. So far back... And now...then...to me. It is fixed in the emotions of all your ancestors. The one who laid the foundation for the road in Herndon, Virginia, and was lashed for laziness as he stopped to wipe the sweat from his brow with this kerchief. Or, your great great grandmother, who covered her face with it, and then covered it with her hands as she rocked and silently wailed, when told that her girl child, barely thirteen, would be sent 'cross the state for breeding purposes. Or the one who leapt for joy on hearing of the Emancipation Proclamation, fifteen years late mind you, only to watch it fall in slow motion from his hand and onto the ground when told that the only job he could now get, was the same one he'd done for free all those years, and now he's forced to take it, for not enough money to buy the food to fill even one man's belly. And more... so much more. What I add to this already fully endowed cloth, will cause you such...... such... Wretchedness. Othe... Othello.

(The contents of the flask have been transformed from violet to clear. BILLIE places the handkerchief onto a large tray. Then with tongs, she takes the hot flask and pours the contents over the handkerchief. She retrieves a vial from the table, opens it.)

My sable warrior... Fight with me. I would fight with you... Suffer with me... I would suffer—

(She starts to pour, but the vial is empty. The buzzer rings. BILLIE is surprised. The buzzer rings again. BILLIE turns off the Bunsen burner. She takes the flask into the kitchen and pours it into the sink. The buzzer rings once more. Going back to the table, she carefully takes the tray and heads toward the bathroom. There is a knock at her door.)

BILLIE :   *(From the bathroom.)* You have a key, let yourself in... Make yourself right at home, why don't you—

MAGI: *(Offstage.)* Billie? Billie, it's me. Magi.

BILLIE: Magi?

MAGI: *(Offstage.)* Are you OK?

BILLIE: Yes. Yes. I'm fine. Let me call you later, OK Magi?

(We hear the sound of liquid being poured. The toilet flushes.)

(MAGI offstage mumbles something about BILLIE having a visitor.)

BILLIE: What?

MAGI: *(MAGI mumbles something about a visitor again.)*

BILLIE: What? Door's open!

> *(MAGI enters and stands in the doorway. She is speaking quietly, as if not wanting someone to hear.)*

MAGI: Sweetie, you have a visitor. Shall I—

BILLIE: *(Entering the living area.)* Look I'm tired. He's been here practically all day already—

MAGI: No, no, no. He said his name is Canada. *(BILLIE turns to MAGI.)* He says he's your father. That's what he said. He said he was your father.

> *(A man in his late sixties, brushes past MAGI. He wears a hat, and has a small suitcase in his hand.)*

CANADA: Sybil? Sybil! There's my girl. Come and give your Daddy a big hug.

(End of ACT I.)

L-R: Alison Sealy-Smith, Barbara Barnes Hopkins, Jeff Jones

ACT II

Scene 1

*(Harlem, present: late summer—night. The cello
and bass pluck and bow a funky rendition of Aretha
Franklin's "Spanish Harlem" against the audio
sound of Michael Jackson and Lisa Marie Presley's
interview on ABC's "Dateline". CANADA is
sitting on one of the chairs, amidst stacks of boxes.)*

CANADA: The first time I came to Harlem, I was scared. Must
have been '68 or '69. Yeh... We we're living in the
Bronx, and your mother was still alive. Everything
I'd ever learned told me that I wasn't safe in this
part of town. The newspapers. Television. My
friends. My own family. But I'm curious, see. I
says, Canada you can't be in New York City and
not see Harlem. So I make my way to 125th. "A"
train. I'm gonna walk past the Apollo, I'm gonna
see this place. I'm gonna walk the ten city blocks
to Lexington and catch the "6" train back, if it's the
last thing I do. So out of the subway, I put on my
'baddest mother in the city' glare. I walk—head
straight. All the time trying to make my stride say,
"I'm mean...I'm mean. Killed somebody mean."
So I'm doing this for 'bout five, ten minutes, taking
short furtive glances at this place I really want to
see, when I begin to realize... No-one is taking any
notice of me... Not a soul. Then it dawns on me: I'm
the same as them. I look just like them. I look like I
live in Harlem. Sounds silly now. But I just had to
catch myself and laugh out loud. Canada, where
did you get these ideas about Harlem from?

(The kettle whistles.)

BILLIE: How do you like it?

(BILLIE heads to the kitchen to make tea.)

CANADA: Brown sugar. No milk.

BILLIE: I don't even know why I asked, I don't have any milk anyway.

CANADA: You can't take milk. Never could. When your mother stopped feeding you from her milk, that cow's milk just gave you colic. And those diapers... Now that's an image I'll never forget.

BILLIE: So what brings you to these parts?

CANADA: Just passing through. Since I was in the neighbourhood, thought I'd stop on in.

BILLIE: Nova Scotia's nearly a thousand miles away.

CANADA: Well, I thought I should see my grandchild. Jenny's almost six and I've only talked to her on the phone. And Andrew and his wife, and you. Nothing wrong with seeing family is there?

BILLIE: Strong or weak?

CANADA: Like a bear's bottom.

BILLIE: Polar or Grizzly?

CANADA: Grizzly.

(BILLIE returns with a tray.)

Andrew told me what happened.

BILLIE: He did, did he?

CANADA: Said you were taking it kinda hard.

BILLIE: Oh, I'll be fine. I'm a survivor. But then again, you already know that.

CANADA: Tea should be ready. Shall I be mother?

BILLIE: Go ahead.

(CANADA pours the tea.)

BILLIE: I hear you were in the hospital.

CANADA: My liver ain't too good. Gave out on me. I guess you reap what you sow.

BILLIE: Still drinking?

CANADA: Been sober going on five years now.

BILLIE: Good. Good for you.

CANADA: Don't mean I don't feel like it sometimes though…

BILLIE: Well… How long do you plan to be in town?

CANADA: Just a few days. See Andrew and his family. See the sights. I'm staying there—at Andrew's. Went by there earlier… No one home. Must have given them the wrong time. Left a note though. Told them to find me at Sybil's.

BILLIE: Billie. I've always despised that name. Sybil.

CANADA: I gave you that name. It's a good name. It was your Grandmother's name. It means prophetess. Sorceress. Seer of the future. I like it. I don't see anything wrong with that name.

BILLIE: Sounds like some old woman living in a cave.

(CANADA reaches for his suitcase.)

CANADA: I brought something for you.

(He takes out a small red box.)

Go on… Open it. The box is a bit too big, but…

(BILLIE opens the box.)

It's your mother's ring. I figured she'd want you to have it.

BILLIE: I hardly remember her anymore. I get glimpses of this ghostly figure creeping in and out of my dreams.

CANADA: When Beryl first passed on, I couldn't get her off my mind, like she'd gone and left us somehow. Left me… With two kids, one a young girl ripening to sprout into womanhood. I was sad, but I was good and mad too. One minute I'd be trying to etch her face into my mind, cause I didn't want to forget. Next thing, I'd be downing another shot of rye… I couldn't carry the weight. I just couldn't do it by myself. That's when we moved to Dartmouth. What's that them old slaves used to say? "I can't take it no more, I moving to Nova Scotia."

BILLIE: I'm thinking of heading back there myself…

(Pause.)

CANADA: 'Cause he left you, or 'cause she's White?

(Pause.)

BILLIE: I remember that White woman… That hairdresser you used to go with… The one with the mini skirts… What was her name?

CANADA: That's going way back… You remember her?

BILLIE: She was boasting about knowing how to do our kind of hair. And she took that hot comb to my head… Sounded like she was frying chicken… Burnt my ears and half the hair on my head. I hated her stubby little beige legs and those false eyelashes. She taught me how to put on false eyelashes.

CANADA: Deborah.

BILLIE: Debbie… Yes… Debbie.

(Pause.)

CANADA: I wish… I wish things between…

(The buzzer rings.)

BILLIE: That must be Drew.

(BILLIE goes to the console by the door.)

Drew?

AMAH: *(Through intercom.)* It's me. Amah. Is your—

BILLIE: He's here. Come on up.

CANADA: You know, an old African once told me the story of a man who was struck by an arrow. His attacker was unknown. Instead of tending to his wound, he refused to remove the arrow until the archer was found and punished. In the meantime, the wound festered, until finally the poison infected his entire body, eventually killing him... Now, who is responsible for this man's death, the archer for letting go the arrow, or the man for his foolish holding on?

> *(There is a knock at the door. BILLIE gets up and heads toward it.)*

BILLIE: The drunk?

CANADA: A drunken man can get sober but a damn fool can't ever get wise.

> *(BILLIE opens the door. AMAH enters with some rolls of paper in her arms.)*

AMAH: *(Kissing BILLIE's cheek.)* Hi sweetie. And you must be Canada.

CANADA: Drew's wife...

AMAH: So very pleased to meet you at last.

CANADA: Delighted...

AMAH: We weren't expecting you until tomorrow. We ate out tonight. We would have come pick you up. Jenny's so excited.

CANADA: No, no... No need to fuss. I arrived safe and sound. And Sybil—Billie's been taking good care of me.

AMAH: Drew would have come himself. Jenny insisted he give her a bath tonight. You know, it's a father-daughter thing.

> *(Silence.)*

Anyway, we should get going. *(To CANADA)* You're probably starving. I can rustle something up for you in no time.

(CANADA reaches for his coat.)

(To BILLIE.) Look, I'm gonna have to bring that child of mine over here. She's driving me crazy asking for you—

BILLIE: No. No….not yet.

AMAH: Well, if I go mad, you and Drew will have to take care of her. I want you to know that. Oh, Jenny asked me to give these to you. She made them specially for you. She wanted to give you some inspiration. You might not be able to tell, but one's of her dancing, and the other's of her singing.

BILLIE: Tell I miss her.

AMAH: I will.

BILLIE: Tell her I'll see her real soon.

AMAH: I will.

BILLIE: *(To AMAH.)* I still have a bone to pick with you, though. *(Indicating CANADA.)*

AMAH: No, no. You have a bone to pick with Drew.

CANADA: I'll drop in again tomorrow, if that's OK with you.

BILLIE: Tomorrow might not be so good. He's moving his stuff in the morning. We'd probably be in the way. I won't even be here until sometime in the afternoon.

CANADA: Well then… We'll see how things go.

(He kisses BILLIE on the forehead.)

AMAH: Come join us over something to eat—

BILLIE: No. Thanks. I'm fine.

CANADA: Good to see you, Sybil—Billie.

BILLIE: Well it certainly was a surprise. Bye y'all.

> *(AMAH and CANADA exit. BILLIE closes the door, then leans against it as she studies the pictures Jenny drew.)*

L-R: Nigel Shawn Williams, Alison Sealy-Smith

Scene 2

(Harlem, the present: the next day—late morning. Lyrical strains give way to an undulating rhythm while Malcolm X recounts the tale of how George Washington sold a slave for a gallon of molasses. The apartment looks empty of furniture, save for the bed, several piles of books, and boxes strewn around the living area. OTHELLO walks into the bedroom with a large green garbage bag. After a few moments, the door is unlocked and BILLIE peers through the doorway. She hears someone in the bedroom. She quietly closes the door behind her and places a small brown paper bag in her pocket. She makes her way into the kitchen area. She waits. OTHELLO exits the bedroom, green garbage bag in tow. He walks to the centre of the living room where he stands for a few moments taking it all in.)

BILLIE: Got everything?

OTHELLO: *(Startled.)* Ahh! *(Dropping the garbage bag, he turns around.)* Christ…

BILLIE: Got everything?

OTHELLO: God, I didn't hear you come in.

BILLIE: My meeting ended earlier than I expected. I was able to get what I needed…I didn't see a van. I figured you'd be done by now.

OTHELLO: They just left. I was doing a final check. See if I'd forgotten anything.

BILLIE: So the move went well.

OTHELLO: Yes…yeh. It's amazing how much stuff there is.

BILLIE: Yeh. It's hard to throw things away.

OTHELLO: I know what you mean. We've got a huge place though.

BILLIE: Good. Good for you.

(*Pause.*)

OTHELLO: This place looks pretty huge right now, though. Remember when we first came to look at this place?

BILLIE: Yes.

(*Pause.*)

OTHELLO: Well... I guess that's it.

BILLIE: I guess...

(*Pause.*)

OTHELLO: Anyway... So when do you plan on leaving?

BILLIE: Oh, I don't... I don't know.

OTHELLO: Ah.

BILLIE: I haven't decided.

OTHELLO: I see... Well...

BILLIE: So when's the big day?

OTHELLO: Oh.....well... Er... Three weeks.

BILLIE: So soon?

OTHELLO: Just a small affair.

BILLIE: Good. Good for you. Good for you both.

OTHELLO: Yeh...

BILLIE: I... I've been meaning... Well...I've been thinking.

OTHELLO: Hmn Hmn...

BILLIE: I...er... I...um... I want to return something you gave me...centuries ago.

OTHELLO: Oh?

BILLIE: The handkerchief?

OTHELLO: Oh! Really? Wow... No. No. It's not necessary. Really—

BILLIE: No, no, let me finish. I've.......been foolish. I understand that now. You can understand why. And......I'm sorry. That's what I wanted to tell you. And the handkerchief...it's yours. Held by me for safekeeping really. To be passed on to our children—if we had any. Since we don't, it should be returned to you, to your line...

OTHELLO: Why are you doing this?

BILLIE: I just thought you might... I thought you would... After all...it's the only thing your mother left you...

OTHELLO: I don't know what to say.

BILLIE: I thought you'd be glad.

OTHELLO: Oh, I'm more than glad.

BILLIE: But I have to find it first.

OTHELLO: Are you sure about—.

BILLIE: I'm sure. Give me a couple of days, to find it...... clean it up a bit.

OTHELLO: I could come by.

BILLIE: Yes. You should have it before... You know... before your...big day.

OTHELLO: Thank you.

BILLIE: Just trying to play my part well.

OTHELLO: Thanks.

BILLIE: Forgive me...

OTHELLO: I know it's been hard.

BILLIE: Yeh..

OTHELLO: OK. Well...

(He reaches to touch her face. She retreats.)

BILLIE: I'll see you in a couple of days then.

OTHELLO: Alright.

BILLIE: Alright.

OTHELLO: Alright. And say Hello to Jenny for me. *(Silence.)* Alright.

(OTHELLO exits. BILLIE takes the small package out of her pocket. She unwraps it, revealing a small vial of fluid. She goes into the kitchen, vial in hand, turns toward the fridge, opens the freezer door and stares into it.)

BILLIE: Look this way and see...your death... Othe... Othe...

(She places the vial into the freezer.)

Scene 3

(Harlem, 1862: late summer—night. Indigo blues groan as if through a delta, while echoes of a presidential voice reads from the Emancipation Proclamation. The sound fades. HER holds HIM in her arms like Mary holds Jesus in Michelangelo's 'The Pieta'. There is a rope around his neck. He does not move.)

HER: *(Caressing him.)* Once upon a time, there was a man who wanted to find a magic spell in order to become White. After much research and investigation, he came across an ancient ritual from the caverns of knowledge of a psychic. "The only way to become White," the psychic said, "was to enter the Whiteness." And when he found his ice queen, his alabaster goddess, he fucked her. Her on his dick. He one with her, for a single shivering moment became...her. Her and her Whiteness.

Scene 4

*(Harlem, present: late summer — night. A cacophony
of strings grooves and collides as sound bites from
the Anita Hill and Clarence Thomas hearings, the
L.A. riots, the O.J. Simpson trial, Malcolm X, and
Martin Luther King, loop and repeat the same
distorted bits of sound over and over again. BILLIE
is alone in the apartment. She goes into the freezer
and removes the vial. Wearing rubber gloves, she
places several drops of a liquid substance onto
the handkerchief. She replaces the cap of the vial.
BILLIE carefully folds the handkerchief, hesitates
for a moment, looks around and spots the red box
on the mantle. She puts the handkerchief back down
on the tray and, with her hands in the air, like a
surgeon scrubbing for surgery, she gets up and goes
to the red box. With one hand she takes off one of
the gloves. With the ungloved hand, she opens the
red box and slips her mother's ring on her finger.
She then takes the red box with her to the table. She
very carefully replaces the one glove, picks up the
handkerchief, and neatly places it in the small red
box. She works slowly, and is mindful not to touch
the sides of the box with the handkerchief itself.*

*She removes a single rubber glove once more, picks
up the cover to the box, and places it on top of the
other half. She is still for a few moments, staring at
the box.*

*BILLIE gets up and crosses the room, as if looking
for something, only to stop in her tracks and return
to the box. She paces. Her pacing appears more
methodical than hysterical. Suddenly she stops. She
turns to look at the small red box.*

She shakes her head and takes a seat on a large, full, cardboard box at her feet. Her breathing becomes more apparent as she begins to rock, almost imperceptibly at first. Finally she places her head in her hands.

After several moments, BILLIE's face slowly emerges from her hands.

She glares at the gloved hand incredulously, as she realizes that she has inadvertently transferred some of the potion onto her own skin. She quickly removes the second glove, and proceeds to wipe her face with her own clothes.)

BILLIE: *(To herself.)* Oh god! Oh my god! Shit! Shit! Shit! Shit!

(BILLIE gets up and rushes to the kitchen sink, turns on the tap and frantically washes her hands and face in the water.)

Scene 5

(The following day: early evening. In counterpoint to the cello and bass, the distorted sound loop becomes a grating repetition. MAGI and CANADA are on either side of a large box, sitting on two smaller ones. The larger box is covered by a scarf to resemble a table cloth, on top of which is a small feast. They are eating. MAGI gets up and goes to the door of the bedroom. She peeks in. After a few moments she closes the door and returns to her seat.)

MAGI: She's in distant realms. I checked in on her when I got back from church. I thought she was speaking in tongues. I couldn't understand a thing she was saying. I don't think she slept a wink all night. Those pills work like a charm, though. *(Beat.)* How is it?

CANADA: Mmn! Those greens... She looks like an angel and cooks like one too.

MAGI: Can I get you some more?

CANADA: No, no, I don't want to appear too greedy now.

MAGI: Here... *(Serving him another helping.)* There you go. And I won't tell a soul. Promise.

CANADA: I haven't tasted cooking like this in a long time.

MAGI: My Mama would say, some food is good for the mind, some is good for the body, and some food is good for the soul.

CANADA: Your Mama taught you how to cook like this?

MAGI: Once she even taught me how to cook a soufflé. She used to have a restaurant downstairs from as far back as I can recall. And I guess the boys returning home from the war in Europe kept asking for the Parisian food, and it ended up on her menu. She'd say, now this Parisian food ain't good for nothing. Soufflé ain't nothing more than baked eggs. And eggs is for breakfast. Eggs don't do no one no good past noon.

CANADA: So you've lived here all your life?

MAGI: And my mother before me, and her mother before her. My great grandmother, worked for the family that lived here, most of her life. She never married, but she had two children by the man she worked for—seems his wife never knew they were his. One brown baby looks just like another to most White folks. And when the wife died, my great grandmother just stayed on. Everybody thinking she's just the maid, but she was living like the queen of the manor—him being her babies' father and everything. And his other children were all grown by then. So when he died, he left everything to his White children, 'cept this house. He left it in my great grandmother's name, and it's been in my family ever since.

CANADA: So the White man's children ever find out? About their brown skinned relatives.

MAGI: I don't know. The Van Dykes—they were Dutch. We used to watch the Dick Van Dyke show, and my Grandmother used to always say, "That there's your relative!" But we didn't pay her too much mind. More greens?

CANADA: If I eat another thing, I will truly burst. This was wonderful. Thank you. Thank you very much.

MAGI: You're more than welcome.

CANADA: When I was a boy, I used to love to sop the pot liquor.

MAGI: It's nearly the best part.

CANADA: You sure know the way to a man's heart.

MAGI: Haven't had any luck so far.

CANADA: Yet.

                  (There is an awkward silence between them, after which they both start speaking at once.)

MAGI: *(Overlapping.)* Well I better get started with these dishes...

CANADA: *(Overlapping.)* I should go in and check on Sybil... Let me give you a hand.

MAGI: No, no, it's quite alright. I can handle this.

                  (BILLIE enters.)

CANADA: Billie! Marjorie was kind enough to share her dinner with me.

MAGI: Billie, come and have something to eat.

BILLIE: I'm not hungry. I heard voices. I need to go back and lay down...get some reading done.

MAGI: You can't have eaten anything for the day, girl.

BILLIE: I'm fine.

CANADA: What you need is a good meal inside you.

BILLIE: I said I was fine.

MAGI: I'll just take these things downstairs.

                  (MAGI exits.)

CANADA: I'll make you some tea, OK.

BILLIE: I don't—don't need any tea. I don't want anything to eat. I'm fine. I'm sorry. I don't—don't—don't mean...to be like this... But I haven't seen you in God knows how long... And you just show up, and expect things to be all hunky dory.

                  (Pause.)

CANADA: Well, I'll be off then.

(He goes for his coat.)

BILLIE: I'm sorry.

CANADA: Me too.

(He heads for the door.)

BILLIE: And I am glad you came... Maybe this can be... You know....like a beginning of something...I don't know.

CANADA: I nearly came before... Two or three times... You know, when I heard. I wished your mother was here. I really wished for her... Her wisdom. I mean Beryl would know what to do. A girl needs her mother. And I know you didn't have her all those times...I mean, I couldn't tell you. What could I tell you? I kept seeing your face. It's your mother's face. You've got my nose. My mouth. But those eyes... The shape of your face... The way you're head tilts to one side when you're thinking, or just listening. It's all her. You've got her moods. I used to call them her moods. Once 'bout every three months, on a Friday, when she'd have the weekend off, she'd come home from that hospital, take off her clothes and lay down in her bed and stay there 'till Sunday afternoon. She'd say she'd done turned the other cheek so many times in the past little while, she didn't have no more smiles for anybody. She'd say, better she just face God and the pillow than shower me and the children with the evil she had bottled up inside her. See, if you spend too much time among White people, you start believing what they think of you. So I'd take you and Drew and we'd go visiting. We'd take the whole weekend and visit all the folks we knew, in a fifteen mile radius... When we'd get home, she'd have cleaned the house, washed the clothes and even made a Sunday dinner. And after I'd pluck the guitar... And she'd start to sing... And you'd dance... You remember? You'd dance. You'd stomp on that floor like you were beating out some secret code to God or something...I know you—we don't see eye to eye. I know you haven't wanted to see very much anything of me lately. But I've known you all your life. I carried you in my arms and on my back, kissed and spanked you when you needed, and I watched you start to talk, and learn to walk, and read and I just wanted to come… I just wanted to come. And I know I can't make everything alright. I know. But I was there when you arrived in this world. And I didn't think there was space for a child, I loved your mother so much. But there you were and I wondered where you'd been all my life, like something I'd been missing and didn't know I'd been missing. And I don't know if you've loved anybody that long. But behind your mother's face you're wearing, I still see the girl who shrieked with laughter, and danced to the heavens sometimes…

(CANADA slowly approaches BILLIE. She does not move. He takes her in his arms. He holds her in his arms for a long time.)

Scene 6

(Harlem, 1928: late summer — night. The strident movement of the strings is joined by the rising tempo of the distorted sound loop. HE and SHE are both in a tiny dressing room, as in the prologue. On a counter is a shaving brush, a straight-edged razor, greasepaint and a top hat. HE wipes his face with a towel. SHE holds the handkerchief out to him. He does not take it. She lets it fall at his feet. After a few moments, he picks it up.)

HE: *(Referring to the handkerchief at first.)* White, red, black, green, indigo... What difference does it make? That makes no sense...makes no difference. "If virtue no delighted beauty lack, Your son-in-law is far more fair than black." Far more fair than black. I want...I need to do this... For my soul. I am an actor. I—

SHE: *(Kindly.)* A minstrel. A Black minstrel...

(He places the towel on the counter beside the toiletries.)

HE: It's paid my way.

(She caresses the towel.)

SHE: Stay, my sable warrior...

(Her hand stumbles upon the razor.)

HE: I'll not die in black-face to pay the rent. I am of Ira Aldrigde stock. I am a classical man. I long to play the Scottish king. The prince of Denmark. "The slings and arrows of outrageous..." Or... Or... "There's a divinity that shapes our ends, Rough-hew them how we will"... Those words... I love those words. They give me life. Mona sees my gift. She's cast me as the prince of Tyre. She's breathed new life into a barren dream. She… She… She has a serene calmness about her. That smile… I bet they named her Mona because even at birth, she had that constant half smile, like the Mona Lisa. Skin as smooth as monumental alabaster… As warm as snow velvet.

(She exposes the blade.)

SHE: My onyx prince…

HE: Ooohh…

(She approaches him from behind.)

SHE: My tourmaline king…

(She leans her head on his back.)

HE: S'alright…

SHE: My raven knight…

(She wraps her arms around him. He turns his head toward her.)

HE: Oh sweet…

SHE: My umber squire…

HE: I wish… I wish—

(Her hand rises, the razor is poised, nearly touching the skin of his neck, just below his ear, within his peripheral vision.)

SHE: My Cimmerian lord…

(He turns around, as if to see what she's holding, and in that turn, his neck appears to devour the blade. The razor's shaft at once hidden by his flesh, swiftly withdraws, leaving a rushing river of red like a scarf billowing around his neck and her hands. He yields to gravity.)

Scene 7

*(Harlem, the present: late summer night. The
plucked strings and the distorted audio loop have
become even more dissonant. BILLIE is clutching
the small red box.)*

MAGI: …You know, Hakim has seven children, and he's
never been married. Brother Hakim. Spot him at
any street rally where the subject is prefaced by
the words "Third World". He's the one with the
"Lumumba Lives" button prominently displayed
on his authentic kente cloth dashi—Billie? Billie,
what's up? You don't look so good.

(Pause.)

Billie?

BILLIE: Sybil. I'm Sybil.

MAGI: That's what your Daddy calls you.

BILLIE: Yes.

MAGI: Your Daddy sure is one good-looking gentleman.

BILLIE: Trapped in history. A history trapped in me.

MAGI: I'm serious. I mean…I wanna know if you mind?
Really. You were still a little girl when your mama
died.

BILLIE: I don't remember Beryl's funeral. I see my father
dressed in black, sewing a white button, on to his
white shirt, with an enormous needle. He attaches
the button and knots the thread so many times
it's like he's trying to hold onto more than just the
button. Like he can't bear for anything else in his
life to leave him.

MAGI: He's a nice man. Would you mind?

BILLIE: Am I nice?

MAGI: Billie, I bet you haven't eaten today.

BILLIE: Can you keep a secret?

MAGI: No, but that's never stopped you before.

BILLIE: Then sorry…

MAGI: OK, OK. I promise.

BILLIE: I am about to plunge into very dangerous waters. Give me your word.

MAGI: You're not going to do something stupid, now.

BILLIE: Your word?

MAGI: Yeh, OK.

BILLIE: I've drawn a line.

MAGI: A line? A line about what?

BILLIE: I'm returning the handkerchief—the one his mother give him. The one he gave to me when we first agreed to be together…

MAGI: I don't understand.

BILLIE: I've concocted something… A potion… A plague of sorts… I've soaked the handkerchief… Soaked it in certain tinctures… Anyone who touches it—the handkerchief, will come to harm.

MAGI: Now that is not a line, Billie, that is a trench!

BILLIE: I'm supposed to…

MAGI: Billie, if this kind of stuff truly worked, Africans wouldn't be in the situation we're in now. Imagine all them slaves working magic on their masters— didn't make no difference. If it truly worked, I'd be married to a nice man, with three little ones by now. But if it makes you feel better—

BILLIE: He's going to marry her... Officially...

MAGI: I know... I know. Remember, what goes around comes around. Karma is a strong and unforgiving force.

BILLIE: I haven't seen it affect White people too much.

MAGI: Is everything about White people with you? Is every living moment of your life is eaten up with thinking about them. Do you know where you are? Do you know who you are anymore? What about right and wrong. Racism is a disease my friend, and your test just came back positive. You're so busy reacting, you don't even know yourself.

BILLIE: No, no, no... It's about Black. I love Black. I really do. And it's revolutionary... Black is beautiful... So beautiful. This Harlem sanctuary......here. This respite... Like an ocean in the middle of a desert. And in my mirror, my womb, he has a fast growing infestation of roaches. White roaches.

MAGI: Billie?

BILLIE: Did you ever consider what hundreds of years of slavery did to the African American psyche?

MAGI: What? What are you...?

BILLIE: Every time someone mentions traditional values or the good old days—who exactly were those days good for?

(The phone rings. BILLIE goes over it. She sits on the bare floor but does not answer.)

Jenny... Is that you Jenny. My beauty. My little girl. It's Sybil... Auntie Sybil... The woman who lives in the cave.

(BILLIE laughs.)

MAGI: I'll get it for you.

(BILLIE picks up the receiver.)

BILLIE: Yes, yes, I'm here. Oh, Othe... Othello. I didn't recognize your voice. You sound......different. No. No, no, you can't pick it up. I mean— I've got it, yes. It's right here. No. No, I won't be in... No, no. I haven't changed my mind. But—I mean... I have to go... Roaches. Yeh, blue roaches. Green roaches. So I have to go now. I—I just have to go.

            (BILLIE replaces the receiver.)

MAGI: He's coming over?

BILLIE: I don't want a Mona Lisa smile...

MAGI: Oh Billie... Billie, you're all in bits and pieces.

BILLIE: I know. I know. A tumour. Suddenly apparent, but its been there, tiny, growing slowly for a long time. What kind of therapy to take? Chop it out? Radiate it? Let it eat me alive? I see roaches all around me. In me. Blue roaches. Green roaches. Aah! Get off! Get it off. I eat roaches. I pee roaches. Help! I'm losing... I don't don't... I'm falling...

MAGI: Billie? Billie?

BILLIE: I have a dream today.

MAGI: You had a dream?

BILLIE: I have a dream that one day every valley shall be engulfed, every hill shall be exalted and every mountain shall be made low...oh...oh...the rough places will be made plains and the crooked places will be made...

MAGI: *(Overlapping.)* It's gonna be alright, Billie.

            (MAGI goes to the phone and dials.)

BILLIE: *(Overlapping.)* ...straight and the glory of the Lord shall be revealed and all flesh shall see it together.

MAGI: *(Overlapping.)* It's Magi. You all better get over here, now. No, no, no. NOW. Alright. Alright.

            (MAGI puts down the receiver and returns to

BILLIE. *She gently takes the red box from out of BILLIE's hands, and places it on the mantel.)*

BILLIE: *(Overlapping.)* ...This is our hope...

MAGI: *(Overlapping.)* It's gonna be alright. I know... I know...

BILLIE: *(Overlapping.)* ...With this faith we will be able to hew out of the mountain of despair a stone of hope...

MAGI: *(Overlapping.)* It's OK. It's OK. Let's start with a little step. Come on. Come with me. *(MAGI helps BILLIE up.)* Come on... Good. Let's get some soup into you. Warm up that frozen blood of yours. *(MAGI leads her to the door.)* Warm up your insides. Come... Come on... Chase all the roaches out...

(BILLIE breaks loose of MAGI and rushes to the window.

MAGI is no longer in the room. OTHELLO appears wearing a brightly coloured dashiki. He is inspecting a broom, laying against the fridge. It is now Fall, seven years earlier. Save for the broom, and the fridge, the apartment is empty.)

BILLIE: Look... Come, look... You can see the Apollo from the window. I love it.

OTHELLO: Where?

BILLIE: Over there. See.

OTHELLO: Oh yeh —If I crane my neck.

BILLIE: I could find some lawn chairs and table and we'd have a city terrace.

OTHELLO: On the fire escape?

BILLIE: We'd have our own little balcony.

OTHELLO: Patio.

BILLIE: Terrace...

OTHELLO: We could buy a house up here.

BILLIE: We can't afford to buy a house until I finish school. If I'm going to go to school full-time, this fall, like we agreed—you'd go to school, then I'd go to school—how can we afford a down payment on a house?

OTHELLO: I know. I know.

(Pause.)

BILLIE: I love it. Don't you love it?

OTHELLO: I love you.

BILLIE: I love you and I love it.

OTHELLO: Think Chris Yago and Mona and the other faculty will feel uncomfortable coming up here...for meetings and the like...

BILLIE: It's on the subway line.

OTHELLO: And boy do they need to take the journey. I'll take them on a cultural field trip—blow their minds.

BILLIE: I've longed for this sanctuary.

OTHELLO: I know what you mean.

BILLIE: Black boutiques.

OTHELLO: Black bookstores.

BILLIE: Black groceries.

OTHELLO: Filled with Black doctors and dentists. Black banks.

BILLIE: Black streets teeming with loud Black people listening to loud Jazz and reggae and Aretha... *(Singing.)* "There is a rose in Spanish Harlem. *(He joins her.)* A rose in Black and Spanish Harlem. Da da da, da da da..." Maybe later we could buy a place on 'strivers row', that's where all the rich Black folks live.

OTHELLO: Strivers row.

BILLIE: Owned by Blacks hued from the faintest gold to the bluest bronze. That's my dream.

OTHELLO: By then you'd have your Ph.D.

BILLIE: And a small lecturer's position at a prestigious Manhattan university. We might even have enough money to get a small house in the country too.

OTHELLO: A big house in the country too?

BILLIE: A big house with a white picket fence.

OTHELLO: On a rolling emerald hill.

BILLIE: I want 2.5 kids.

(He kisses her lightly.)

OTHELLO: You're mad, you know that.

BILLIE: That makes you some kinda fool for loving me, baby.

OTHELLO: Let's do it. There's an old broom right over there. Wanna jump it with me?

(OTHELLO retrieves the broom.)

BILLIE: Are you asking me to m—

OTHELLO: Yes… Yes, I am asking.

BILLIE: Yes… *(Silence.)* Then yes.

(OTHELLO kisses her. He places the broom in the middle of the floor. He takes BILLIE's hand. They stand in front of it.)

What will we use for rings?

OTHELLO: Think them old slaves had rings? Slave marriages were illegal, remember. This broom is more than rings. More than any gold. *(He whispers.)* My ancient love.

BILLIE: *(She whispers.)* My soul.

(OTHELLO kisses her hand. The couple gaze at each

other, preparing to jump over the broom. They jump.
They hold each other. The landlady enters.)

MAGI: Oh—I'm sorry.

BILLIE: No, no. We were just...just—

(OTHELLO picks up the broom and places it to one side.)

OTHELLO: I think we'll take it.

MAGI: I didn't mean to rush you. I can give you another few minutes if you need to make good and sure?

BILLIE: I think we're sure. *(To OTHELLO.)* You sure? *(To MAGI.)* We're sure.

(MAGI looks gravely at BILLIE. They are the only ones in the room. We are back in the present. MAGI carefully approaches BILLIE. BILLIE stares at where OTHELLO stood, only moments ago.)

MAGI: Come on. Come with me. Come on... Good. Let's get some soup into you. Warm up that frozen blood of yours. *(MAGI leads her to the door.)* Warm up your insides. Come...come on... Chase all the roaches out... One by one... One by one...

(They exit.)

L-R: Barbara Barnes Hopkins, Alison Sealy-Smith

Scene 8

(Harlem, present: late summer, afternoon. A lyrical rhapsody swings to the sound of a commentator describing the scene at the Million Man March. The apartment is virtually empty. CANADA is cleaning the kitchen, taking tubs and bags from out of the freezer. He gives them a brief once-over and then throws them into the trash. OTHELLO enters.)

OTHELLO: Billie? Billie?

CANADA: Othello! Othello, good to see you son.

(They shake hands.)

Good to see you.

OTHELLO: I didn't know... When did you get here?

CANADA: A few days.

OTHELLO: Billie didn't say a word.

CANADA: Well, Billie's in...she's... Billie's not here right now.

OTHELLO: *(Scanning the apartment.)* Did she leave anything for me. An envelope... A package—

(He sees the red box on the mantel.)

Oh. Maybe...

(He goes over to it.)

CANADA: Oh, she said no one was to touch that... I'm supposed to throw it out.

OTHELLO: Great! *(He opens the red box and takes out the handkerchief.)* It's OK, this is it. It's mine. This is what I was looking for.

CANADA: I was just about to throw it in with the trash from the fridge.

OTHELLO: Just in time, huh?

CANADA: Yeh, some of this stuff's about ready to crawl out by itself.

OTHELLO: I can imagine.

CANADA: I swear, one thing had actually grown little feet.

OTHELLO: Well, Billie wasn't one for cleaning... I guess neither of us was.

(There is an awkward silence between them.)

Well... I should be off.

(He takes some keys from out of his pocket and places them where the red box was laying.)

CANADA: She tells me you're getting married.

OTHELLO: I do confess the vices of my blood.

CANADA: I'm real sorry it didn't work out... Between you and Billie... I mean... I was hoping...

OTHELLO: Yes. I know.

CANADA: She's my child, so—

OTHELLO: I know, I know.

CANADA: You young'uns don't know the sweetness of molasses... Rather have granulated sugar, 'stead of a deep clover honey, or cane sugar juice from way into the Demerara. Better watch out for that refined shit. It'll kill ya. A slow kinda killin'. 'Cause it kills your mind first. So you think you living the life, when you been dead a long time.

(Silence.)

OTHELLO: Well sir...I should be somewhere.

CANADA: *(Nodding.)* Well, I hope we can catch up sometime...

(OTHELLO goes to the door.)

OTHELLO: That would be great. Tell Billie I came by.

CANADA: I'll tell her that. She'll be glad to know.

OTHELLO: Good seeing you.

CANADA: You too...son... You too.

(OTHELLO takes one last look at the apartment, takes out a tiny cellular phone, and exits. CANADA is still for a few moments. From the hallway we hear OTHELLO.)

OTHELLO: *(Offstage.)* Chris Yago, please.

(CANADA returns to the fridge, and continues to clean.)

Scene 9

(Harlem, 1928: late summer—night. The music softly underscores the voice of Paul Robeson speaking about not being able to get decent acting roles in the U.S., and how fortunate he feels to be offered a contract to play OTHELLO in England. HE is alone. He proceeds to cover his face in black grease paint. He begins to speak, as if rehearsing, at first.)

HE: It is most true; true, I have married her.
It is most…
It is most true; true, I have married her.
For know, but that I love the gentle Desdemona,
(She) questioned me the story of my life
From year to year—the battles, sieges, fortunes,
That I have passed. These things to hear
Would Desdemona seriously incline;
But still the house affairs would draw her thence,
Which ever as she could with haste dispatch
she'd come again, and with a greedy ear
Devour up my discourse. Which I, observing,
Took once a pliant hour…
And often did beguile her of her tears,
When I did speak of some distressful stroke
That my youth suffered…

(In the background we can hear a children's song. HE begins to add a white greasepaint to his lips, completing the mask of the minstrel.)

…My story being done,
She gave me for my pains a world of sighs.
She wished she had not heard it, yet she wished
That heaven had made her such a man. She thanked me,
She thanked me…
She thanked me…
She thanked me…

Scene 10

(Harlem, the present: late summer—night. A ber-yline blues improvisation of "Mama's Little Baby" cascades alongside a reading of the Langston Hughes poem "Harlem". AMAH sits beside BILLIE in the visitors lounge of the psychiatric ward. AMAH is clearly saddened by BILLIE's state.)

BILLIE: *(Singing.)* ...Step back Sal-ly, all night long.
Strut-in' down the al-ley, al-ley, al-ley,
Strut-in' down the al-ley, all night long.

AMAH
& BILLIE: I looked over there, and what did I see?
A big fat lady from Ten-nes-see.

(BILLIE gets up and begins to dance.)

I bet you five dollars I can beat that man,
To the front, to the back, to the side, side, side.
To the front, to the back, to the side, side, side.

(The two women laugh.)

BILLIE: I haven't done that in...in years.

AMAH: I never knew that one—I just saw Jenny do it the other day.

BILLIE: I even remember the dance. *(Singing under her breath.)* ...Bet you five dollars I can beat that man...

AMAH: It's not so bad here.

BILLIE: You'd think the doctors at Harlem hospital would be Black. Especially in psychiatrics. Most of the nurses are Black.

AMAH: But they're nice to you—the doctors?

BILLIE:	They help. I don't—don't want anymore pills. And that's OK. They don't really understand, though. I had this dream. Lucinda—she's my main doctor. Lucinda was sitting at the edge of a couch and I asked her a question. But she couldn't answer because her eyes kept flashing. Like neon lights. Flash, flash, flash. That was it. That was the dream. I knew it was important, but I didn't get it. And I told her. And she didn't get it either. But it gnawed away at me... For days... The flashing eyes. And that was it! The eyes were flashing blue. Her eyes were flashing blue. She could only see my questions through her blue eyes.
AMAH:	Something in you really wants to heal.
BILLIE:	Exorcism.
AMAH:	Pardon?
BILLIE :	Repossess.
AMAH:	Self-possession?
BILLIE:	I hate. I know I hate. And he loves. How he loves.
AMAH:	Billie?
BILLIE:	Why is that, you think?
AMAH:	Some of us spend our entire lives making our own shackles.
BILLIE:	Canada freedom come.
AMAH:	And the experienced shackle-wearer knows the best polish for the gilt.
BILLIE:	I wanna be free.
AMAH:	It must be hard, though. I feel for him.
BILLIE:	I'm not that evolved.
AMAH:	Forgiveness.
BILLIE:	Forgiveness...

AMAH: If I don't forgive my enemy, if I don't forgive him, he might just set up house, inside me.

BILLIE: I just … I—I despise—I know…I know… Moment by moment. I forgive him now. I hate— I love him so—I forgive him now. And now.

           (She moves as if to speak, but stops herself.)

           And I forgive him now.

AMAH: My time's up, sweetie.

BILLIE: I have a dream…

AMAH: Sorry?

BILLIE: I had a dream…

AMAH: Yes… I know.

BILLIE: Tell Jenny… Tell her for me… Tell her that you saw me dancing.

AMAH: I will tell her.

BILLIE: And tell her… Tell her that you heard me singing.

AMAH: I will.

BILLIE: And tell her… I'll see her real soon.

AMAH: I will tell her, Billie. I will tell her.

           (AMAH kisses BILLIE on the cheek and begins to exit. CANADA enters.)

BILLIE: *(In the background softly.)*

           Betcha five dollars I can beat that man.
           To the front, to the back, to the side, side, side.
           To the front, to the back, to the side, side, side.

CANADA: How's she doing?

AMAH: Mmm, so-so.

CANADA: Okay. Thanks.

AMAH: We'll really miss you when you go—back to Nova Scotia.

CANADA: Oh, I don't think I'm going anywhere just yet— least if I can help it. Way too much leaving gone on for more than one lifetime already.

> (BILLIE *stops singing for a moment, then segues into a version of Aretha Franklin's "Spanish Harlem", more hummed than sung.*
>
> CANADA *pats* AMAH *on the back.* AMAH *turns and exits.* CANADA *approaches* BILLIE *and sits down beside her.*
>
> *Shortly, he joins her in the song. He rests his hand on hers.*
>
> *After several moments: The lights fade to black.)*

The End